John B. Dunlop

The 2002 Dubrovka and 2004 Beslan Hostage Crises

A Critique of Russian Counter-Terrorism

With a foreword by Donald N. Jensen

SOVIET AND POST-SOVIET POLITICS AND SOCIETY

ISSN 1614-3515

Recent volumes

John B. Dunlop

THE 2002 DUBROVKA AND 2004 BESLAN HOSTAGE CRISES

A Critique of Russian Counter-Terrorism

With a foreword by Donald N. Jensen

ibidem-Verlag
Stuttgart

Bibliografische Information der Deutschen Nationalbibliothek
Die Deutsche Nationalbibliothek verzeichnet diese Publikation in der
Deutschen Nationalbibliografie; detaillierte bibliografische Daten sind im
Internet über http://dnb.d-nb.de abrufbar.

Bibliographic information published by the Deutsche Nationalbibliothek
Die Deutsche Nationalbibliothek lists this publication in the Deutsche Nationalbibliografie;
detailed bibliographic data are available in the Internet at http://dnb.d-nb.de.

Frontcover picture: Beslan's School No. 1 on 18 September 2004.
© Tanya Lokshina
Editorial assistance: Joyce Cerwin and Elena Sivuda

A CIP catalogue record for this book is available from:
Die Deutsche Bibliothek
http://dnb.ddb.de

∞

Gedruckt auf alterungsbeständigem, säurefreien Papier
Printed on acid-free paper

ISSN: 1614-3515

ISBN: 3-89821-608-X

© *ibidem*-Verlag
Stuttgart 2006
Alle Rechte vorbehalten

To the children of Beslan and Dubrovka

Contents

Permissions

Abbreviations

APC   Armored Personnel Carrier

FSB   *Federal'naya sluzhba bezopasnosti* (Federal Security Service)

GAI   *Gosudarstvennaya avtomobil'naya inspektsiya* (State Automobile Inspection)

GRU   *Glavnoe razvedovatel'noe upravlenie* (Main Intelligence Directorate)

GUBOP   *Glavnoe upravlenie po bor'be s organizovannoi prestupnost'yu* (Main Directorate for Combating Organized Crime)

KGB   *Komitet gosudarstvennoi bezopasnosti* (Committee of State Security)

MUR   *Moskvoskii ugolovnyi rozysk* (Moscow Criminal Investigation)

MVD   *Ministerstvo vnutrennikh del* (Ministry of Internal Affairs)

NTV   *Nezavisimoe televidenie* (Independent Television)

NVF   *Nezakonnoe vooruzhennoe formirovanie* (Illegal Armed Formation)

OMON   *Otryad militsii osobogo naznacheniya* (Specialized Designation Police Detachment)

PChG   Psycho-chemical gas

RIA   *Rossiiskoe informatsionnoe agenstvo* (Russian Information Agency)

RPG   *Reaktivnyi protivotankovyi granatomet* (Recoilless Anti-tank Grenade Launcher)

RPO   *Reaktivnyi pekhotnyi ognemet* (Recoilless Foot Soldiers' Flamethrower)

RSO-A   *Respublika Severnaya Ossetiya – Alaniya* (Republic of North Ossetiya – Alania)

RTR   *Rossiiskaya teleradiokompaniya* (Russian Radio and TV Company)

RUBOP   *Regional'noe upravlenie po bor'be s organizovannoi prestupnost'yu* (Regional Directorate for Combating Organized Crime)

SOBR   *Spetsial'nye otryady bystrogo reagirovaniya* (Special Rapid-Reaction Units)

Spetsnaz   *Spetsial'nogo naznacheniya* (Special Designation [Forces of the Interior and Border Troops])

SVR   *Sluzhba vneshnei razvedki* (Foreign Intelligence Service)

TsRU   *Tsentral'noe razvedovatel'noe upravlenie* (Central Intelligence Agency)

UBOP   *Upravlenie po bor'be s organizovannoi prestupnost'yu* (Directorate for Combating Organized Crime)

UFSB RF   *Upravlenie Federal'noi sluzhby bezopasnosti Rossiiskoi Federatsii* (Directorate of the Federal Service for Security of the Russian Federation)

UVD   *Upravlenie vnutrennikh del* (Directorate for Internal Affairs)

VTsIOM   *Vserossiiskii tsentr izucheniya obshchestvennogo mneniya* (All-Russian Center for the Study of Public Opinion)

Foreword

Nothing more exemplifies the agony of Russia's post-Soviet transition than its bloody, inconclusive involvement in two wars in Chechnya. Russian troops entered Chechnya in December 1994 in order to prevent that region's efforts to secede from the Russian Federation. Tens of thousands of civilians were killed during two years of fighting and over 500,000 persons displaced. Human rights organizations in Russia and abroad denounced the indiscriminate use of force by Russian forces.

The origins of the conflict lay in several factors. First, the Chechens had never recognized the forcible incorporation of their land into the Czarist Empire in the 19th century. Often demonized in the public mind as congenitally criminal, Stalin deported thousands to Central Asia during World War II.

Second, Chechnya was strategically vital to Moscow due to the access it offered to the Black Sea and the oil and gas pipelines that run through it from Azerbaijan and Central Asia to the Russian heartland. Finally, Chechen President President Dzhokhar Dudaev was prepared to use the general disintegration of federal authority after the end of the Soviet Union to remove Chechnya from the Russian Federation entirely. This was intolerable to the Kremlin, which was struggling to hold the country together.

A peace agreement, reached in 1996, provided that resolution of Chechnya's call for independence would be postponed for at least five years. The stalemate had shown the incompetence of the Russian military and highlighted President Yeltsin's erratic leadership. The role played by public opinion and a freer press, both largely against the war, gave hope that Russian's leaders were now popularly accountable.

In the following three years, Chechnya degenerated into a lawless place of crime, corruption and violence. Shamil Basaev, a prominent field commander during the 1994-96 war, was named Acting Chechen Prime Minister in November 1997. By early 1998 Basaev had emerged as the main radical secessionist opponent of the Chechen president, Aslan Maskhadov, who in his opinion "was pushing the republic back into the Russian Federation." In mid-year, Basaev was appointed deputy commander of the republic's armed forces, which he used to tap into swelling support for radical Islam within the North Caucasus.

Under circumstances that have never been fully explained, armed Islamic extremists based in Chechnya staged incursions into neighboring Dagestan in August and September 1999. Their goal, they claimed, was to establish a breakaway Islamic state. Vladimir Putin, Russia's newly appointed prime minister, responded militarily. Russian forces drove the invaders out of Dagestan and entered Chechnya. The political timing was perfect for the previously little known Putin, who overnight became widely seen by voters as a young, tough leader who would stand up to Chechen terrorism. He rode a wave of popular support to the Russian Presidency.

Despite early military successes, Russian troops became again bogged down, much as they had in the first conflict, in inconclusive fighting marked by chaos, misinformation, ignorance and widespread civilian casualties. The widespread trade in oil and arms by both sides raised doubts that anyone was in charge.

After the terrorist attacks on New York City on September 11, 2001, the Russian government made linkage of the war in Chechnya with the global fight on terrorism a central tenet justifying the war. Thus, unraveling what actually happened during the 2002 Dubrovka and 2004 Beslan hostage crises, which the Kremlin linked with international terrorism, is central to understanding not only what has happened in that tragic region, but why the fighting continues.

No scholar is better able to sort out what really occurred than John Dunlop, whose scholarly rigor and sensitivity to all sides enables him to sort fact from propaganda. For these reasons, I commend his impressive studies of these two events to everyone interested in a reconciliation of the Chechen and Russian peoples.

Donald N. Jensen
Director of Communications
Radio Free Europe/Radio Liberty

I Beslan: Russia's 9/11? [1]

"In my presence three shots were fired from a tank located in the court-yard into the school. I asked: 'What are you doing?' They answered: 'There are rebels.' I responded: 'But there are people there too.'"

Stanislav Kesaev
Chair of the North Ossetiyan parliamentary commission on Beslan[2]

According to official Russian statistics, in the period between 1-3 September 2004, 330 individuals perished in a terrorist incident at School Number 1 in the town of Beslan in the Republic of North Ossetiya in southern Russia. Of those who died, 317 were hostages—186 of them children. Ten were soldiers from the Russian FSB *spetsnaz* (special forces), two were personnel from the Russian Ministry for Emergency Situations, while one was a resident of Beslan who was killed while helping to evacuate the hostages during the storming of the building. Seven hundred and twenty-eight persons were said to have received wounds.[3] A majority of the hostages who died—more than 160—perished under the collapsed roof of the school.[4]

---

[1] The author would like to thank Robert Otto for a number of bibliographical sugges-tions and for helpful comments on a draft of this report. Glen Howard of the Ameri-can Committee for Peace in Chechnya and Christopher Swift of ACPC and the Uni-versity of Cambridge both made numerous valuable comments on the draft. Law-rence Uzzell also made useful suggestions on the draft. Finally the author would like to express his gratitude to his research assistants, Joyce Cerwin and Yuliya Shmeleva, for their fine work.

[2] Vremya.ru, 28 June 2005.

[3] Ol'ga Allenova, "Byli deistviya, kotorye byli pokhozhi na shturm," *Kommersant-vlast'*, 29 August 2005.

[4] Statement of Stanislav Kesaev, chair of the commission of the North Ossetiyan par-liament to investigate the Beslan events, in "Vlast' dolzhna otvechat' za svoyu be-spomoshchnost'," Gazeta.ru, 1 September 2005.

This horrific terrorist event, occurring on the first day of a new school year, represented, according to two reporters for the *Washington Post*, "clearly the worst terrorist attack in the world since September 11 [2001]."[5] It also attracted significant international attention. On the first anniversary of the terrorist attack, Russian foreign minister Sergei Lavrov handed to the chairwoman of the North Ossetiyan parliament, Larisa Khabitsovaya, 770,000 signatures under a "Beslan Appeal," collected in 112 countries.[6] Most of the signatures came from residents of former union republics of the USSR. Among the signatories were heads of states and parliamentarians.

Sources

The author of this report was encouraged by several of his colleagues to take a close look at what had occurred at School No. 1 in Beslan at the beginning of September 2004. Given the vastness and complexity of this event, I have chosen to focus on several key questions upon which the Russian General Procuracy and the residents of North Ossetiya have often been in sharp disagreement.

Among the hundreds of documents and press analyses examined by the author in preparing this report, the following are particularly worthy of note. First, there is a draft report on the Beslan incident written by a Russian parliamentary commission headed by Aleksandr Torshin, a deputy speaker of the Federation Council. The Torshin Commission, which includes both Duma deputies and senators from the Federation Council, wrote a draft report whose text was obtained by journalist Elena Milashina of the pro-democracy twice-weekly newspaper *Novaya gazeta*. While Torshin and other members of this

---

5   Peter Baker and Susan Glasser, *Kremlin Rising: Vladimir Putin's Russia and the End of Revolution* (New York, NY: Scribner, 2005), p. 34. The six authors of a lengthy investigative report, entitled "Putin's Ground Zero," in *Der Spiegel*, No. 53, 27 December 2004, pp. 65-101, refer to it as "the bloodiest attack since 11 September 2001."

6   "770,000 chelovek podpisali 'Beslanskoe vozzvanie,'" Gazeta.ru, 1 September 2005.

commission gave a number of rather frank interviews to the Russian press in the early stages of their investigation, they had, by the summer of 2005, generally been reined in by the Kremlin and its supporters. The commission's draft report largely repeats the findings of the Russian State Procuracy, and it should thus be considered an "in-house" investigation. "The commission was supposed to have met with Vladimir Putin this summer, but now the head of the commission, deputy speaker of the Council of Federation Aleksandr Torshin, states that the report may not be completed before the end of this year [2005]."[7]

A second commission, headed by Stanislav Kesaev, a deputy speaker of the North Ossetiyan parliament, has pressed ahead with its own independent investigation of the Beslan events. Its conclusions frequently differ from those of the Russian Procuracy and of the Torshin Commission. The Kesaev commission's draft report was, like that of the Torshin commission, summarized by journalist Elena Milashina on the pages of *Novaya gazeta*. She also compared and contrasted the conclusions of the two commissions.[8]

The Mothers of Beslan, an organization of mothers of children who perished at the school, headed by Susanna Dudieva, has also conducted its own investigation into the events of 1-3 September. Its spokeswomen have given a number of interviews to the Russian and foreign press. The findings of the Mothers are generally quite similar to those of the Kesaev Commission. On 2 September 2005, four of the Mothers were invited to Moscow to meet with President Putin to discuss the events in Beslan.

A Russian deputy procurator general, Nikolai Shepel', summarized his office's preliminary findings at the trial of Nur-Pasha (Nur-Pashi) Kulaev, the lone terrorist whom the Russian authorities claim to have captured at Beslan. Shepel' presented these preliminary findings at a session held at the Supreme Court

---

7   "Beslanskaya komissiya temnit," Gazeta.ru, 7 September 2005.
8   For summaries of the draft reports of both the Torshin and Kesaev commissions, see Elena Milashina, "Den' neznaniya," *Novaya gazeta*, 1 September 2005.

of North Ossetiya on 17 May 2005.[9] The transcripts of the sessions of the Kulaev trial, which contain detailed testimony by former hostages and eyewitnesses among the townspeople, constitute an invaluable source of information concerning the Beslan incident.

Several press reports also deserve mention. First there is an exceptionally
valuable three-part report authored by journalist Svetlana Meteleva, a correspondent for the newspaper *Moskovskii komsomolets*, which cites important
classified documents that had been leaked to her.[10] In a statement given to
Ekho Moskvy Radio, Meteleva's newspaper colleague Aleksandr Minkin
noted that, "the [official Russian] investigation is demanding that the journalist
reveal her sources of information." In Minkin's presence, a federal investigator
directly threatened Meteleva. "After all," the investigator said, "we will find
them [Meteleva's sources] no matter what, and we will punish them."[11]

Also worthy of mention are a number of exceedingly useful investigative articles by the afore-mentioned journalist Elena Milashina that were published in
Novaya gazeta. These path-breaking articles are acknowledged in the foot-
notes throughout this report. There is also a valuable journalistic investigation
that was conducted by six German reporters who fanned out to conduct interviews at key points in North Ossetiya, Ingushetiya and Chechnya in the af-
termath of the Beslan tragedy.[12] Finally, the work of a leading independent
Russian military affairs specialist and journalist, Pavel Felgengauer, is also
noteworthy. Felgengauer early on raised many of the questions—for exam-

---

[9]   See "Pervoe zasedanie Verkhovnogo suda Severnoi Osetii po delu Kulaeva," 17
      May 2005, pp. 6-17. Transcripts of the 39 sessions of the trial held through mid-
      November 2005 may be found at the website: www.pravdabeslana.ru. References
      to these sessions will be provided in shortened form, with a roman numeral used to
      indicate the session and the appropriate page number then being provided, e.g., I,
      6-17.

[10] Svetlana Meteleva, "Beslan bez grifov," parts I-III, *Moskovskii komsomolets*, Mk.ru,
      24-26 May 2005.

[11] "V 'Moskovskom komsomol'tse' soobshchili o doprose avtora stat'i pro Beslan,"
      Lenta.ru, 3 June 2005.

[12] Uwe Buse, Ullrich Fichtner, Mario Kaiser, Uwe Klussmann, Walter Mayr and Chris-
      tian Neef, "Putins Ground Zero," *Der Spiegel*, No. 53, 27 December 2004, pp. 65-
      101.

ple, the issue of whether or not the Russian forces that stormed the school had employed, inter alia, *Shmel'* flamethrowers—that were subsequently posed by both the Kesaev Commission and the Beslan Mothers.[13]

Advance Warnings

A first issue needing elucidation is whether or not the Russian and North Ossetiyan authorities had advance notice of a planned assault on the town of Beslan. On 18 August 2004, nearly a fortnight before the tragedy occurred,

> the Russian Ministry of Internal Affairs sent a telegram to all regional police commandants. It said that there were indications that Chechen rebels were planning an operation in North Ossetiya. It was said to resemble the one that Shamil Basaev once launched at a hospital in the city of Budennovsk in the summer of 1995.... Government buildings, police stations, and train stations [were put] under much closer watch, but the main emphasis was on hospitals and main traffic arteries.[14]

The telegram seems to have neglected the possibility that terrorists who had once struck at a hospital might choose to attack a school.

In early 2005, similar questions arose during a meeting of Beslan residents with Dmitrii Kozak, the plenipotentiary Russian presidential representative in the Southern Federal District. One of the townspeople, Valiko Margiev, told Kozak:

---

[13]   See two interviews with Felgengauer, "Operatsiya spetssluzhb po osvobozhdeniyu zalozhnikov byla oshibkoi," Russian translation of a contribution to *Die Welt*, 7 September 2004, in Inosmi.ru, 7 September 2004; and Jeremy Brantsen, "Troubling questions remain about bloody Beslan siege," *Radio Free Europe/Radio Liberty*, Rferl.org, 6 September 2004. See also: Pavel Fel'gengauer, "'Shmel' i 'svin'i,'" *Novaya gazeta*, 7 October 2004.

[14]   Buse, Fichtner, Kaiser, Klussmann, Mayr and Neef, "Putins Ground Zero."

> On 28 August there stood traffic policemen [GAI] at all the
> crossroads in Beslan. When they began carefully to search
> my vehicle, I asked: 'What has happened?' They answered
> me: 'A group of rebels has penetrated into Beslan.' On 1
> September the police should have been at the school in or-
> der to ensure the security of the children as they crossed
> the road. But they weren't there.[15]

Kozak's response was to keep silent.

At 5:00 a.m. on 1 September 2004, the day on which the school was seized,
a report was sent to the Russian Minister of Internal Affairs, Rashid Nurgaliev,
stating: "Information is being processed concerning the fact that on 1 September 2004 at 5:00 a.m. in the city of Shali [Chechnya], a citizen named Ar-
samikov was taken into custody. During the course of the interrogation Ar-
samikov related that a seizure was planned [that day] of a school in the city of
Beslan."[16] Noting that there are only four schools in the town of Beslan, journalist Svetlana Meteleva then apostrophizes her reader: "Now you model the
situation. You have information that a terrorist act is being prepared, and you
know the time and place of the future act. You still have four hours and five
minutes and special communications equipment. Can you convey this information to the special services in Beslan?" The MVD failed to act on accurate
intelligence.

Despite credible warnings concerning an impending terrorist attack, School
Number 1, with its large number of students and teachers, was left completely
undefended on opening day, 1 September 2004—a ceremonial occasion in
which a number of parents traditionally accompany their children to school.
When El'brus Nogaev, the head of the investigations department of the
Beslan police, who lost his entire family in the school, was asked: "Were sufficient measures taken by the [law enforcement] organs to protect the school

---

[15] Yurii Safonov, "Korpunkt v Beslane: Khodoki," *Novaya gazeta*, 3 February 2005.
[16] Svetlana Meteleva, "Beslan bez grifov," part III, Mk.ru, 26 May 2005.

from being seized?" he replied indignantly, "No of course not. There was no one there except for one [unarmed] woman instructor."[17]

Not only were there no armed police in the school building, there were also no armed traffic police [GAI] parked in vehicles near the school, as had been the practice in recent years. As one eyewitness has recalled: "I have been taking my children to school for five years. Every day I met the GAI at the crossroads. Near the First School, near the school boarding house, and so on. This year there was not a single GAI officer there. I even knew them by name... Where were the GAI? Why wasn't the school being guarded?"[18] Another former hostage asked angrily: "Who removed the GAI posts? Who removed the police from the school? There was no guard there. There was one policewoman without a telephone and without a gun."[19]

According to deputy procurator General Nikolai Shepel', the responsibility for the absence of police protection for the school lay with the director of the Pravoberezhnyi District Department of the Interior Ministry of North Ossetiya, Miroslav Aidarov, and two of his subordinates, Taimuraz Mukrtazov and Guram Dryaev. Although they had received instructions from their superiors "to take the relevant measures due to the threat of terrorist attacks on 1 September," they chose, Shepel' said, to ignore these orders and instructions. Two officers who were supposed to have served as armed security at the school "were sent off to the Caucasus Highway [supposedly] to guard the president of North Ossetiya."[20] It was later revealed that President Dzasokhov of North Ossetiya had had no travel plans for that day.

The lone unarmed policewoman who was in the school when it was seized, Fatima Dudieva, was asked: "Can you say why on that day, 1 September,

---

[17]   Zaur Farniev, "Po nam terroristy voobshche ne strelyali," *Kommersant*, 15 June 2005.

[18]   Pravdabeslana.ru, X, 52.

[19]   *Ibid.*, XII, 6.

[20]   Nikolai Gritchin, "The actions of police officers in Beslan helped the terrorists," *Izvestiya*, 11 November 2004. English translation in *Johnson's Russia List*, No. 8448, 11 November 2004.

they did not leave one or two [GAI] police cars next to the school?" Dudieva responded: "They said that they never have enough people. They had to protect the highway because a high-ranking official was due to pass by. Until now, however, they haven't been able to figure out who he was supposed to be."[21]

Was the absence of police protection due merely to disorganization and incompetence or to other factors? During the time that the hostages were being held in the school building, a deputy leader of the terrorists, Vladimir Khodov, mocked them, boasting aloud: "Your police sold you out for $20,000."[22] The payment of a hefty bribe to the police could quite conceivably have contributed to the absence of any armed protection at the time that the terrorists struck. It should also be noted that Shamil Basaev, the terrorist leader who was in titular command of the assault on the school, has claimed that he tricked the Russian authorities into leaving the school unprotected because they thought that he planned to attack government buildings in North Ossetiya. While conceivable, this boastful claim by a notorious liar seems less likely than the payment of a large bribe.

A Trail Run for Beslan

A number of those who have looked into the Beslan events have concluded that the roots of the assault on the school lie in the bloody events of 21-22 June 2004 that occurred in the Republic of Ingushetiya. "Shamil Basaev," one journalist has noted, "thought up this operation, as a result of which 80 persons were killed and 106 wounded, with 57 of the killed and 51 of the wounded being employees of law enforcement organs. The main goal of the attackers was to add to their stores of weapons and ammunition... About forty of the attackers stole 1,177 firearms and 70,922 bullets."[23] Several days after the Beslan events, Russian deputy procurator general Vladimir Kolesnikov

---

[21]   Pravdabeslana.ru, XIII, 39.

[22]   *Ibid.*, XVIII, 34.

[23]   Yuliya Kalinina, "Lyubimyi gorod mozhno sdat' spokoino," Mk.ru, 22 June 2005.

announced that "seven automatic weapons and three pistols" used by the terrorists in the school had come from an MVD armory in Ingushetiya raided on 21-22 June.[24]

Shamil Basaev and his top confederates released a video message following this assault on police stations and armories in Ingushetiya. "I want to say thanks to the MVD of Ingushetiya for keeping these weapons for me," Basaev boasts mockingly on the film.[25] Appearing with Basaev on the film is a bearded man bearing a strong physical resemblance to "the Colonel," the terrorist who, all sources agree, led the assault on the school building at Beslan. Another figure, whom Russian law enforcement personnel have identified as an Arab named Abu Dzeit, asks the Colonel on the film: "Are you ready to meet Allah?" The colonel replies: "I am ready."[26] Russian procurators, including deputy procurator general Nikolai Shepel', subsequently asserted that this film was made just before the assault on Beslan. That information was demonstrably misleading—the film was made in June of 2004, not in late August.[27]

The June raid on Ingushetiya is related to Beslan in another important respect. One of the demands of the terrorists at Beslan, as we shall see, was that some 30 or so of their confederates who had been arrested following the events of 21-22 June be released from prison.

Preparing the Raid

During the trial of captured terrorist Nur-Pasha Kulaev, a number of former hostages and local townspeople presented evidence showing that the terror-

[24]   "Oruzhie dlya terakta v Beslane ukrali u ingushskoi militsii," Lenta.ru, 10 September 2004.

[25]   Svetlana Meteleva, "Otmorozhennyi Magas," Mk.ru, 15 April 2005.

[26]   Nick Paton Walsh, "Mystery still shrouds Beslan six months on," *The Guardian*, 16 February 2005. For a discussion of three Ingush police officers who allegedly assisted Basaev in carrying out the June raid, see Musa Muradov, "Informatora Shamilya Basaeva likvidirovali dvazhdy," *Kommersant*, 24 August 2005.

[27]   "Naidena zapis' podgotovki terakta v Beslane," Gzt.ru, 1 September 2005.

ists had in fact had access to the school before the events of 1-3 September. It was claimed, for example, that the terrorists had concealed a number of weapons in the school in advance of the assault.[28] It was even asserted that the terrorists had been able to construct an elaborate sniper's nest fortified with bricks and sandbags in the attic of the school above the gymnasium.[29] It was also claimed that one group of terrorists had been in Beslan for at least a week before the terrorist incident and that one of them—a man with a highly visible large scar across his neck from ear to ear—had been seen in the market place the previous Sunday.

There are also indications that an advance group of terrorists effectively took command of the building on the night from 31 August to 1 September, before it was attacked by the main group after 9:00 a.m. that morning. That is, for example, the contention of policewoman Fatima Dudieva, who was seized on the second floor by terrorists as the building was being raided from outside[30]. All such claims by former hostages and townspeople have been heatedly rejected by the Russian Procuracy.

For his part, Russian deputy procurator general Nikolai Shepel' has insisted: "The rebels brought their weapons with them. In addition, from the testimony of the victims we learned that the repair work on the school was conducted with the help of the local administration and that no other persons participated in the repairs."[31] This was not always, it should be noted, the position of official Russian spokespersons. On 4 September 2004, FSB general Valerii Andreev, head of the North Ossetiyan secret police, announced that "weapons and explosive materials were carried in and hidden on the territory of the school" before the terrorist event occurred.[32]

---

[28]   Pravdabeslana.ru, VIII, 15, XII, 25, XIII, 27, XVI, 20.

[29]   Elena Milashina, "Vyshe nekuda," *Novaya gazeta*, 5 September 2005.

[30]   Pravdabeslana.ru, XIII, 34. On the alleged complicity of the school's watchwoman, Zarema Digurova, in the terrorist attack, see "Beslantsy obvinyayut storozha shkoly v sgovore s boevikami," *Nezavisimaya gazeta*, 18 November 2005.

[31]   "Zamgenprokurora zayavil, chto shturma v Beslane ne bylo," Newsru.com, 3 September 2005.

[32]   "Osnovnuyu chast' oruzhiya i vzryvchatki v shkolu terroristy zavezli zaranee," Vazhno.ru, 4 September 2004.

In June of 2005, the German newspaper *Die Welt* reported that a former hostage, Kazbek Dzarasov, had admitted publicly that he had been forced by three "unknown persons" dressed in camouflage uniforms to give false testimony at the trial of Nur-Pasha Kulaev. According to *Die Welt*, Dzarasov "was forbidden [by them] to say that when he was a hostage the terrorists had forced him to open up the floor of the building and extract weapons hidden there, obviously long before the tragedy."[33]

One point, however, seems unambiguous: the terrorists brought with them a detailed floor plan of the school. As Aleksandr Torshin, the head of the Russian parliamentary commission, has remarked: "They [the terrorists] were precisely going to Beslan. And precisely to school No. 1. Khuchbarov ['The Colonel'] had in his pocket a floor plan of the school, and that has been firmly established."[34] The attack was premeditated.

According to the investigative team of *Der Spiegel*,

> The men and women who later invaded Beslan had assembled in the woods southwest of the village [of Psedakh in Ingushetiya] since 20 August. The terrorists were spartanly equipped and well-acquainted with living in the forest.... The hostage-takers had been recruited from the 'Riyad al-Salihin' (Garden of the Righteous) Martyrs' Brigade. The brigade made its first appearance during the hostage-taking at Moscow's Nord-Ost musical theater [in October 2002]... Che-

---

[33] "Troe neizvestnykh v kamuflyazhe ugrozhali zalozhniku Beslana, i on dal na sude lozhnye pokazaniya," Newsru.com, 23 June 2005. *Die Welt* also reported that a male teacher who had died in the school conveyed the same information to a female hostage. At a session of the Kulaev trail on 27 September 2005, former hostage Sarmat Khudalov asserted that he and other hostages had been forced to extract weapons and ammunition from under the floorboards of the school. See "Byvshii zalozhnik v Beslane rasskazal, kak ego zastavlyali dostavat' spryatannye pod polom boepripasy," Newsru.com, 27 September 2005. See also: "Byvshaya zalozhnitsa: terroristy zaranee zavezli i khranili oruzhie pod polom v beslanskoi shkole," Newsru.com, 29 September 2005.

[34] "'Shmelei ot komissii ne spryachesh,'" *Moskovskie novosti*, 11 February 2005.

chen field commander Shamil Basaev...is the martyr brigade's self-proclaimed emir.[35]

Questions have been raised, quite appropriately, as to why the Ingush police,
who, after the bloody events of 21-22 June, had been on a high terrorism
alert, failed to spot this large gathering of terrorists. As the *Der Spiegel* team
notes: "In the weeks before the attack, when the perpetrators were making
preparations in an Ingushetiya woodland, the [Ingush] police had several op-
portunities to act—but nothing happened."[36] The Russian General Procuracy
announced in November 2004 (and then, again, in September 2005) that it
was charging the two top Ingush police officials of Malgobek District of Ingushetiya with "criminal negligence" for failing to report the presence of the
terrorists. But was it criminal negligence or was it something else?

As the terrorists drove from the woodland of Psedakh in Ingushetiya to the
school in Beslan they "approached the Ossetiyan Cossack village of Staryi
Batakoyurt via a good road. There are four police posts... Normally it takes
just a handful of rubles to get by the controls."[37] Outside the village of Khurikau, in North Ossetiya, the terrorists took captive—at least that is the victim's
version—an ethnic Ingush policeman named Sultan Gurazhev who had
stopped their vehicle. Amazingly, this policeman was subsequently let go by
the terrorists once they arrived at the school at Beslan. According to the testimony of accused terrorist Nur-Pasha Kulaev, "They didn't kill the policeman
at Khurikau on the order of the Colonel. The Colonel said: 'That is the brother
[i.e., cousin] of one of ours.'"[38]

Shortly after 9:00 a.m., the main group of the terrorists, led personally by the
Colonel, firing automatic weapons in the air, expertly rounded up some 1,200
hostages and herded them into the school building. As they were doing that,
a second group of terrorists apparently finished securing the building. After
hearing from a parent that a suspicious vehicle was in the vicinity, unarmed

---

[35]   Buse, Fichtner, Kaiser, Klussmann, Mayr and Neef, "Putins Ground Zero."

[36]   *Ibid.*

[37]   *Ibid.*

[38]   Meteleva, "Otmorozhennyi Magas."

policewoman Fatima Dudieva realized that she needed to call headquarters: "I ran up to the second floor of the school [where there was a telephone]. As soon as I tried to pick up the phone, I was surrounded by 9-10 rebels in light-colored camouflage uniforms, and they said: 'Lady cop, whom are you trying to call? This will not be a Nord-Ost.'"[39]

"How did they turn out to be on the second floor?" Dudieva was asked at the Kulaev trial. "What do you mean 'turn out'?" she responded. "They had been there the entire night."[40] Dudieva also noted that the group of terrorists who seized her had warmly embraced the members of the main group of rebels when they ascended the stairs to the second floor. "Yes," she recalled, "they embraced when they met. And they showed by their expressions that everything was excellent. They [the terrorists] were comprised of several groups; I think that was the case."[41]

Following their successful seizure of the school building, the terrorists, again led by the Colonel, began setting up an elaborate network of explosive devices in the school gymnasium, where the great majority of the hostages were being held. Openings were knocked out in the upper parts of the windows so that the there would be ventilation and, more importantly, so that the Russian *spetsnaz* could not launch a gas attack as they had done at Nord-Ost. All cell-phones were confiscated from the hostages.

The Terrorist Leaders

In his televised report to President Putin on 9 September 2004, Russian procurator general Vladimir Ustinov singled out two of the terrorists for special mention: "their leader, who was called 'the Colonel,'" and "one of the rebels who was called Abdul..."[42] Former hostages also highlight the roles of these

---

[39]   Pravdabeslana.ru, XIII, 34. At Nord-Ost some of the hostages had used cell-phones to contact the authorities.

[40]   Pravdabesdlana.ru, XIII, 36.

[41]   *Ibid.*, XIII, 41.

[42]   "Versiya genprokurora," Vremya.ru, 9 September 2004.

two men. One of the women hostages recalled several days after the storming of the school: "One of them was called 'Abdulla,' and it was evident that they related to him with respect, but they related with still greater respect and honor to the one whom they called 'the Colonel.'"[43]

Concerning the man known by the code-name "Abdul" or "Abdulla," there exists a virtual surfeit of information. It is known that "Abdul'" was an ethnic Ukrainian convert to Islam whose real name was Vladimir Khodov. Khodov had been born in 1976 in Ukraine to an ethnic Ukrainian mother who spoke Russian at home. Nothing is known about his Ukrainian birth-father. When Vladimir was three years old, he was brought by his adoptive father, an ethnic Ossetiyan serving in the Soviet army as an engineer who was fifteen years older than Vladimir's mother, to the town of El'khotovo in North Ossetiya. Shortly thereafter the couple had a son of their own, whom they named Boris.

The town of El'khotovo represents a kind of Muslim bastion in largely Orthodox Christian North Ossetiya. It boasts a large mosque but does not have an Orthodox church. From an early age, therefore, Vladimir was exposed to Muslim influences. He grew up speaking Russian without the local Ossetiyan accent, but he also became fluent in Ossetiyan.[44] A key turning point in Vladimir's life occurred in 1995, when his sixteen-year-old brother Boris was arrested and then sentenced to eight years in prison for having committed a murder: he had stabbed a neighbor to death during an argument. Boris "shared a cell with a group of Muslims and converted to Islam. Khodov visited his brother in prison, and, under his influence, converted too."[45]

On one occasion, in 1998, when Vladimir had traveled to the town of Maikop to visit his brother, he himself committed a serious crime, the rape of a young

---

[43]   Ruslan Pliev, "Obeshchali ubit' zalozhnikov i smyt'sya v Chechnyu," Gazeta.ru, 9 September 2004.

[44]   For Khodov's biography, see Buse, Fichtner, Kaiser, Klussmann, Mayr and Neef, "Putins Ground Zero;" Elizaveta Maetnaya, Marina Gridneva, "Pozyvnoi Abdulla," Mk.ru, 7 September 2004; Mark Franchetti and Matthew Campbell, "How a repressed village misfit became the butcher of Beslan," *Sunday Times* [UK], 12 September 2004.

[45]   *Sunday Times* [UK], 12 September 2004.

woman. Following the commission of this crime, Vladimir found himself on the Russian wanted list. In 2003, Khodov's brother was released from prison, a year ahead of time, but he immediately got himself into trouble again. Having kidnapped a young woman who had caught his fancy, Boris was then shot dead by the woman's brother. A number of residents of El'khotovo have recalled that, even though he was on the Russian wanted list, Vladimir showed up for his brother's funeral, which was held on 22 July 2003, insisting that Boris be given a Muslim funeral. While he was in town, "Khodov told neighbors that he was studying to become a mullah at an Islamic institute in Dagestan." "It was clear," one villager recalled, "that he had become a fanatic. He tried to convert us to Islam. He told us that the only true religion was Islam."[46]

Despite the fact that he was on the Russian wanted list, Vladimir spent the days and weeks following his brother's funeral in El'khotovo at the home of a local Muslim known as Hadji Ali. It was at this point that, "The police, the sixth division of the North Ossetiyan Ministry of Internal Affairs, arrested him but [then] released him straight away."[47] The police even offered him a lift home.[48] Why this benevolent treatment of a wanted rapist on the part of the North Ossetiyan police? The journalistic team of *Der Spiegel* speculated that Khodov managed to pay a large bribe to the police in order to obtain his release. Russia's most wanted terrorist, Shamil Basaev, on the other hand, has claimed that Khodov was not arrested on this occasion not because he had paid a bribe but because he had agreed to become a police agent. "He was offered a choice: prison with its resulting [homosexual] rape or to go to work for them."[49] Khodov was given the police agent's code-name "Traveler" [*Putnik*]. Eventually, according to Basaev, Khodov became an agent of both RUBOP (the anti-organized crime division of the regular police which has an anti-terrorist subsection) and the FSB.

---

[46]   *Ibid.*

[47]   Buse, Fichtner, Kaiser, Klussmann, Mayr and Neef, "Putins Ground Zero."

[48]   Franchetti and Campbell, "How a repressed village misfit became the butcher of Beslan."

[49]   Shamil Basaev, "U nas mnogo, chto rasskazat' po Beslanu...," *Kavkaz Tsentr*, 30 August 2005, posted at Chechenpress.info, 31 August 2005.

Following his release by the police, Khodov soon emerged as a deadly terrorist. On 3 February 2004, together with some Ingush confederates, he set off a car bomb in Vladikavkaz, North Ossetiya, aimed at killing students who were studying at a local school for MVD internal troops. One student was killed in the blast and ten were wounded, while a passerby was also killed.[50] Khodov's photograph was then widely circulated by the police. Despite his growing notoriety, however, Khodov continued to pay regular visits to his hometown of El'khotovo: "Although at this point [February 2004], he was the subject of two arrest warrants (for terrorism, murder and rape) Khodov still moved about freely in his hometown of El'khotovo in the spring and summer of 2004. But the local police chief, Lieutenant Colonel Valerii Dzhibilov, did not order his arrest."[51]

In May of 2004, Khodov stepped up his terrorist activities. On the twenty-ninth of that month: "At 7:27 a.m., train No. 35 from Moscow to Vladikavkaz went off the rails as a result of two explosions near the station of—pay attention!—El'khotovo. Only by a miracle were none of the 463 passengers on board not hurt. The same kind of bomb was used as had been employed in Vladikavkaz."[52] Yet despite these brazen terrorist acts, "For an entire month and a half [in the summer of 2004] Khodov walked quietly about his native village wearing a [Muslim] prayer cap and was from morning till night in the mosque."[53] While he was in El'khotovo, Khodov stayed at the home of his mother. "The entire Ossetiyan police force," investigative journalist Aleksandr Khinshtein has observed sardonically, "exhausted itself looking for Khodov. And during this time he...was living peacefully at his home [in El'khotovo]. This was established by correspondents from *Moskovskii komsomolets* who visited the village."[54]

Following the terrorist attack on Beslan, some of Khodov's fellow villagers wrote an angry letter to the newspaper *Komsomol'skaya pravda*. On 7 Sep-

---

50   "Pozyvnoi Abdulla," Mk.ru, 7 September 2004.
51   Buse, Fichtner, Kaiser, Klussmann, Mayr and Neef, "Putins Ground Zero."
52   "Pozyvnoi Abdulla."
53   *Ibid.*
54   Mk.ru, 21 October 2004.

tember, they noted, the newspaper had reported that "the special services had been looking for Abdulla for about a year." They then declared:

> We are indignant: the special services were seeking that monster but could not find him. If they had come to our village, we could have told them everything about him... [After his brother's funeral] the police (sixth division, Vladikavkaz UVD) took him into custody and then let him go! Why? After that, he committed a terrorist act in Vladikavkaz, and they again could not find him! We, his fellow villagers, saw him in the mosque, he visited his mother, but the special services couldn't find him! Or they didn't want to?[55]

Several days after the Beslan incident had concluded, a well-known defector from the FSB who currently lives in London, retired lieutenant colonel Aleksandr Litvinenko, hypothesized: "Most likely Khodov, who was being sought on a charge of terrorism, was not arrested at his place of residence in connection with the fact that he was a secret agent of the FSB..."[56] As has been noted, Shamil Basaev offers a similar explanation for the bizarre behavior of the police. Both the secret police and UBOP, he writes, wanted Khodov to become a close associate of Basaev himself. "In order to gain my trust, they helped him to set off several explosions in Vladikavkaz as a member of an Ingush group. Then Khodov, at the behest of the special services of Rusnya [a pejorative term used by Basaev for Russia], proposed to us a Shakhid operation involving the seizure of the parliament and government of North Ossetiya."

This Russian plot failed to achieve its aim, Basaev remarks, because Khodov had decided to become a double agent.

> Having lived about a month among the mujehedin in Ingushetiya, Khodov himself confessed to the Amir of the group

---

[55] "Abdulla dazhe svoemu otsu zhelal smerti," *Komsomol'skaya pravda*, 18 September 2004.

[56] "A. Litvinenko: Lichnosti terroristov na 100% dokazyvayut uchastie FSB v zakhvate shkoly v Beslane," Chechenpress.info, 8 September 2004.

[presumably 'the Colonel'] that he was an agent of the special services (RUBOP and FSB) and that he had been infiltrated with the aim of getting close to me. I met with him, thanked him for his sincerity, and proposed to him that he henceforth work for the good of Islam by becoming a double agent.[57]

Khodov, Basaev reports, accepted the offer.

From the statements of former hostages, we know that Khodov, a criminal and an abusive sadist, was in charge of the more than one thousand people imprisoned in the school gymnasium. "In the gymnasium everyone was directly subordinated to [Khodov]..."[58] (For a photograph of Khodov, see the 6 September 2004 issue of *Komsomol'skaya pravda*.[59]) It is not clear, however, whether or not Khodov was killed during the storming of the school building. In December of 2004, Aleksandr Torshin confided to the newspaper *Moskovskii komsomolets*: "Before me is the result of the coroner's report: 'Khodov, Vladimir [it says] has been identified from his fingerprints and from identification by his mother.' But this comes from the site of the MVD of the Russian Federation, from the most recent days: 'Khodov, Vladimir Anatol'evich, is on the federal wanted list.' So has he been killed or is he being sought?"[60]

Nine months later, in September 2005, the head of the North Ossetiyan parliamentary commission investigating the Beslan incident, Stanislav Kesaev, made the same point: "Khodov, who 'supposedly' was identified [among the dead terrorists], was for several months on the wanted list web site of the MVD. So I ask myself the question: was he killed or not?"[61] Journalists have raised similar questions. Writing in the 12 September 2004 issue of the *Sun-*

---

57   Basaev, "U nas mnogo...," Chechenpress.info, 31 August 2005. In August 2003, the Russian MVD created anti-terrorist center "T" within the Main Administration for the Struggle with Organized Crime (GUBOP). See "Rossiiskaya sistema predotvrashcheniya teraktov: spustya god posle Beslana," Politcom.ru, 17 September 2005.

58   Pravdabeslana.ru, IX, 8.

59   URL: http://www.kp.ru/daily/23354/31826/print/

60   "Drugaya voina," Mk.ru, 22 December 2004.

61   "Ubitogo boevika Khodova eshche neskol'ko mesyatsev razyskivalo MVD," Ej.ru, 1 September 2005.

day Times, Mark Franchetti and a co-author reported: "The authorities said they captured only two [terrorists] alive. One of them was Khodov."[62] On 6 September 2004, the Russian government newspaper *Rossiiskaya gazeta* reported the words of Sergei Fridinskii, deputy procurator general of the Russian Federation for the Southern Federal District: "On suspicion of participating in the seizure of hostages three persons have been taken into custody, including one woman. One of those taken into custody is on the federal wanted list."[63]

The newspaper *Izvestiya* reported that Russian *spetsnaz* who had participated in the storming of the building told the newspaper that "they succeeded in taking four rebels alive, including one woman." Lev Dzugaev, the head of the information-analytical department of the President of North Ossetiya, stated that "three living terrorists" had been taken into custody.[64]

"A North Ossetiyan police spokesman," the *Sunday Times* reported, "claimed Khodov had been captured alive. He went on to explain that the terrorist had committed suicide the following day in his cell. 'You understand,' he added, 'that is the official version.'"[65]

Deputy Russian general procurator, Vladimir Kolesnikov, has, in sharp contrast, insisted that Khodov was in fact killed during the storming of the school. "The first of the destroyed terrorists to be identified was the corpse of precisely Khodov," he declared.[66]

Significantly less is known concerning the man referred to as "the Colonel" [*Polkovnik*], who was unquestionably the leader of the terrorists who seized the school. It should be noted that it took a while for Russian law enforcement

---

[62] Franchetti and Campbell, "How a repressed village misfit became the butcher of Beslan."

[63] Andrei Sharov, "Nelyud' s chernym pogonom," Rg.ru, 6 September 2004.

[64] "Genprokuror ne vse dolozhil prezidentu: neskol'ko terroristov skrylis' iz shkoly," Newsru.com, 9 September 2004.

[65] Franchetti and Campbell, "How a repressed village misfit became the butcher of Beslan."

[66] "Khronika terrora—2004," Strana.ru, 11 January 2005.

to identify him. Immediately after the Beslan tragedy, it was initially reported in the Russian and Western media that the leader of the raid had been thirty-year-old Ali Taziev, an ethnic Ingush and a former senior lieutenant (until 1998) in the external security division of the pro-Moscow police of Ingushetiya.[67] Taziev was said to have been one of the leaders of the June 2004 assault on police departments and police armories in Ingushetiya. Then, on 20 September 2004, Russian deputy procurator general Vladimir Kolesnikov announced that the leader of the terrorists had in fact not been Taziev but rather another ethnic Ingush, Ruslan Tagirovich Khuchbarov, born on 12 November 1972.[68]

Like Khodov, Khuchbarov had a tumultuous and heavily criminalized past. In 1996, he moved from his native town of Galashki, in Ingushetiya, to the city of Orel in southern Russia, where he reportedly "went to restaurants, lived with women, drank vodka and amused himself with narcotics."[69] In 1998, he murdered two Armenians living in Orel in a dispute over a woman.[70] Following this double murder, he, like Khodov, was placed on the Russian wanted list. He then decided to join the ranks of the Islamic terrorists. In September of 2003, he is said to have provided explosives for an attack on a building of the FSB in Ingushetiya which claimed three lives. He is also reported to have participated in an armed attack on a column of Russian troops outside of Galashki and to have been involved, either actively or logistically, in the large-scale 21-22 June 2004 raid on Nazran' and other population centers in Ingushetiya.[71]

---

[67]   "Raskryta lichnost' 'Polkovnika,' rukovodivshego zakhvatom shkoly v Beslane," Newsru.com, 10 September 2004; Tom Parfitt, "Ex policeman 'masterminded Beslan terror,'" *Sunday Telegraph*, 12 September 2004.

[68]   "Zagadka polkovnika," Mk.ru, 20 September 2004; "Dos'e na beslanskikh ubiits," Utro.ru, 24 September 2004; Buse, Fichtner, Kaiser, Klussmann, Mayr and Neef, "Putins Ground Zero."

[69]   Lyudmila Butuzova, "'Razvelos' polkovnikom," *Moskovskie novosti*, 22 October 2004.

[70]   *Ibid.*

[71]   Buse, Fichtner, Kaiser, Klussmann, Mayr and Neef, "Putins Ground Zero;" *Moskovskie novosti*, 22 October 2004.

Unlike in the case of Khodov, the Russian police appear to have made several good faith but bungled attempts to arrest Khuchbarov:

> He routinely got away from security forces: once during an attempt to meet his girlfriend in the Kabardinian city of Nalchik; then again, in 2002, when he escaped the police during a shootout at the bus stop in the Ingushetiyan settlement of Sleptsovskaya; and another time, when he was visiting his father in Galashki and fled into an adjacent corn field to evade approaching police.[72]

When interviewed by reporters for *Der Spiegel*, Khuchbarov's father, Tagir, a retired tractor driver, recalled: "For ten years intelligence officers have come to see me every week... They ask about my sons. Or rather, only about Ruslan, since they shot my younger son, Bashir, in the woods two years ago." A friend of the family in Galashki, Musa Arapkhanov, told *Der Spiegel* that "the 'Colonel' was in Galashki this year [2004], to attend a memorial service for his deceased mother." Arapkhanov added: "He is a very devout man..."[73]

While the investigative journalists of *Der Spiegel* chose to accept the authorities' identification of Khuchbarov as "the Colonel"—and while that identification is likely correct—there remain a few questions that need to be addressed. Although the Russian authorities have insisted that "the Colonel" was called only "Rustam" or "Rasul" by his fellow terrorists, it is certain that he was called "Ali" by his fellow rebels at the school in Beslan. This was confirmed, inter alia, by a medical doctor among the hostages, Larisa Mamitova, who was required by circumstances to hold frequent conversations with "the Colonel." "Among themselves," the newspaper *Russkii kur'er* reported in November 2004, "the bandits [at Beslan] called him Ali."[74] The name issue may not, in the final analysis, mean much of anything. In negotiations with representatives of the Russian authorities, "the Colonel" also called himself "Shakhid" and "Sheikhu." In the presence of former Ingushetiyan president

---

[72] Buse, Fichtner, Kaiser, Klussmann, Mayr and Neef, "Putins Ground Zero."

[73] *Ibid.*

[74] Elena Shesterina, "Fantom po imeni Magas," Ruskur.ru, 5 November 2005.

Ruslan Aushev, he was called "Amir" by his fellow terrorists. Film footage obtained by CBS Television that shows conditions in the school at the time of Ruslan Aushev's visit on 2 September provides an excellent still photograph of the terrorist leader. This photograph could presumably be used to settle any lingering questions there might be concerning the "the Colonel's" identity.[75]

Asked about the Colonel's ethnicity and language abilities by the procurators at his trial, Nur-Pasha Kulaev responded as follows:

> *What was the Colonel [ethnically]?*
> [Kulaev:] The Colonel was an Ingush....
> *In the school when you were there in what language did they give commands?*
> In Ingush. The Colonel [he added] also spoke fluently in Chechen.
> *Did you understand him when he gave commands in Ingush?*
> No, I didn't. But he knew Chechen well...
> *Who in the school decided who should stand where?*
> The Colonel and one other Ingush.[76]

Kulaev also recalled that the Colonel and Ruslan Aushev had spoken in Ingush at the time of the latter's visit to the school.[77]

Numerous descriptions of "the Colonel" given by former hostages revealed an extremely competent but also sadistic terrorist. He was the only one of the terrorists at Beslan seen carrying about a portable sniper's machine-gun such as those used by the Russian *spetsnaz*. In negotiations with representatives of the Russian government, he invariably repeated the same cynical answer,

---

[75]   For the photograph, see this URL: http://www.utro.ru/articles/print/2005/01/24/399651.shtml

[76]   Pravdabeslana.ru, III, 38.

[77]   *Ibid.*, III, 10.

"The hostages do not want food or water. They are on a hunger strike against the [Russian] government."[78] One female hostage has recalled:

> He [the Colonel] behaved himself in the hall aggressively. He conducted himself very badly. He told the children he had come there not to joke around. And when the children asked him, 'May I go to the toilet?' he answered: 'I'm not your uncle, I'm a terrorist. I cannot let you do whatever you want. I also have children. I came here not simply to make jokes. I came here to kill.' I remember that very well.[79]

And indeed, under "the Colonel's" leadership, the terrorists proceeded to execute twenty-one male hostages during the first two days of the incident.

One female hostage, the nurse Larisa Tomaeva, has recalled that the Colonel told her: "They [the Russian forces] killed my whole family, almost my entire line." He then enumerated them, adding, "They cut them all down. Why then should I spare you? I came here to kill."[80] If "the Colonel" was in fact Ruslan Khuchbarov, as the Russian authorities maintain, then this statement constituted a lie. Though he had reportedly lost a brother, Khuchbarov's entire family had not been killed off by the Russians.

It seems likely that "the Colonel," like the de facto leader of the terrorists at Nord-Ost in October 2002, "Abubakar," managed to escape during the storming of the school. "Do you know why I cut my beard?" he asked one hostage. "So I can pass your blockade."[81] In mid-September, one of the Russian investigators of the Beslan incident told the newspaper *Kommersant*: "The Colonel himself did not want to die. We know that on Friday morning [3 September] he divided the rebels into two groups. Into one [i.e., the designated sacrificial

---

78   Buse, Fichtner, Kaiser, Klussmann, Mayr and Neef, "Putins Ground Zero."
79   Pravdabeslana.ru, VIII, 17.
80   *Ibid.*, XIII, 13.
81   Peter Finn and Peter Baker, "Hostages were helpless in the face of chaos," *Washington Post*, 5 September 2004.

lambs] he included people who had in general accidentally found themselves among the rebels."[82] The other group, the elite, were to escape.

That the Colonel succeeded in getting away seems probable. In an interview given in December 2004, Aleksandr Torshin commented that none of the leaders of the terrorists had been identified among the bodies of the dead. Those identified, he said, "are 'small fry.'"[83] When one former hostage, Svetlana Dzebisova, was asked whether she had recognized "Ali" in the photographs taken by the authorities of the dead terrorists, she replied, "No, I did not see him there."[84]

The web-site Ingushetia.ru reported in January of 2005 that Khuchbarov was back with Shamil Basaev fighting in the mountains of Chechnya.[85] On the occasion of the first anniversary of the Beslan tragedy, journalist Vadim Rechkalov wrote on the pages of Moskovskii komsomolets: "Basaev became Basaev after Budennovsk. We were unable to catch him, and now there is a new bandit of world level—Ruslan Khuchbarov—the Colonel—the very one who came to Beslan, did what he wanted there, and safely got away.... If we haven't caught Basaev, then we also won't catch Khuchbarov."[86] The Mohammed Atta of Russia's 9/11 appears thus to be still at large.

The Terrorist Rank-and-File

Who were the rank-and-file terrorists at Beslan? How many of them were there? The Russian Procuracy has stubbornly clung to the version of Nur-Pasha Kulaev that there were 32 terrorists in the band that assaulted the school. At his trial, Kulaev repeatedly claimed to have heard this figure from the Colonel himself shortly before the terrorist attack was launched. "Who said that there were 32 [terrorists]?" Kulaev was asked at the trial. "The Colo-

---

82   Cited in "Beslan: Boeviki shli na delo sem'yami," Grani.ru, 16 September 2004.

83   "Drugaya voina," Mk.ru, 22 December 2004.

84   Pravdabreslana.ru, VIII, 17.

85   "Stat'ya v nemetskom 'Shpigele,'" Ingushetiya.ru, 14 January 2005.

86   Vadim Rechkalov, "Tol'ko tak my pobedim, vraga...," Mk.ru, 14 September 2004.

nel counted them, he said it," Kulaev replied.[87] In his initial interrogation by the Russian authorities on 4 September, however, it emerged during the trial, Kulaev stated that he did not know how many rebels there were in the group.[88] It is therefore possible that the number 32 was first suggested by interrogators and not by Kulaev himself.

Many of the hostages and their relatives believe that there could have been as many as fifty terrorists in the school, perhaps seventy. Writing in the weekly *Kommersant-vlast'*, journalist Valerii Panyushkin reports on a walk he took about the ruined school with the father of a child who had perished in the building. "The school is big," he writes, "we walk about it for a long time. Sasha [last name not given] relates where the rebels stood and, from his explanations, it emerges that 32 rebels could not in any way have controlled this space. So there must have been more rebels, and many of them must have gotten away."[89]

In a similar vein, journalist Yurii Kotenik reported:

> It seems that it remains unclear up until now [February 2005] how many terrorists there were in all at Beslan. School No. 1 consisted of several buildings, separate auditoriums, auxiliary rooms (a boiler room, etc.) and an interior courtyard. One has to take into account that a part of the terrorists had to keep the hostages under the barrels of their guns in the gymnasium, a part had to rest, and a part had to patrol the perimeter and the approaches. Thirty-two terrorists (the number announced by the General Procuracy) simply could not control such a broad territory and such a large number of hostages.[90]

"According to my calculations," stated former hostage Veronika Salkazarova, "and I conducted such calculations from the very beginning, there were not

---

[87]   Pravdabeslana.ru, III, 22.
[88]   *Ibid.*, XI, 31.
[89]   Valerii Panyushkin, "My khotim dokazat', chto vlasti vinovaty v gibeli detei," *Kommersant-vlast*, 28 February 2005.
[90]   Yurii Kotenok, "Za Beslan nakazali 'pomoshchnikov strelochnika,'" Utro.ru, 21 February 2005.

less than 50 persons [among the terrorists], because they constantly spelled each other off."[91] The policewoman who was a hostage in the school, Fatima Dudieva, who impresses one as an attentive observer, has remarked: "There were not less than seventy of them, and they periodically spelled each other off."[92]

The issue of the number of the terrorists cropped up during President Putin's discussion with four Beslan Mothers on 2 September 2005. The chairwoman, Susanna Dudieva, recalls:

> We said that we do not agree that a single group [of 32 rebels] arrived with weapons and seized the school. The president said, 'I have witnesses.' We said that we have other witnesses and that there a great many of them. He said: 'We'll sort this out.' On the question of weapons he has a report [spravka] that there were no weapons in the school [before the raid]. We said that there are other witnesses who can show the opposite.[93]

The *Der Spiegel* investigative team has written that it believes that 32 terrorists, and not 31, were killed at Beslan: "There [were] 32 bodies, which contradicts the official report of 31 dead terrorists. There are 32. An entire platoon of firefighters sees them lying there and swears to the number. There are numbers on the body bags, 1 through 32."[94]

The terrorists' ethnicity represents another key question. It has generally been believed in the West that the Beslan school was attacked by a band consisting mainly of ethnic Chechens. This impression appears to be false. Stansilav Kesaev, the chair of the North Ossetiyan parliament's commission to investigate the Beslan incident, has asserted that the "overwhelming major-

---

[91]   Tat'yana Lokshina, "Pepel Beslana stuchit v moe serdtse," Polit.ru, 27 September 2004.

[92]   Pravdabeslana.ru, XIII, 39.

[93]   "Vladimir Kolesnikov," *Novaya gazeta*, 12 September 2005.

[94]   Buse, Fichtner, Kaiser, Klussmann, Mayr and Neef, "Putins Ground Zero."

ity" of the terrorists at Beslan were ethnic Ingush.[95] It seems likely that future researchers will conclude that Kesaev is correct. As we have seen, according to Nur-Pasha Kulaev's testimony, "the Colonel" and his still unidentified deputy were both ethnic Ingush, and when the Colonel addressed the terrorists he did so in the Ingush language. The Russian authorities also seem to have concluded that they were dealing with a largely Ingush group: leading former top-level Ingush politicians—whom the Kremlin dislikes—like Ruslan Aushev and Mikhail Gutseriev were rushed into service as negotiators.

When asked by prosecutors, "What nationality were the 32 persons in your group?" Nur-Pasha Kulaev responded:

> Ingush, one Arab and one Ossetiyan [presumably Khodov], and one slant-eyed person. The remainder were Ingush and Chechens. There were four or five Chechens...
> *What was the slant-eyed one? A Korean, Chinese, Kazakh?*
> I don't know.
> *Were there [ethnic] Russians among them?*
> There were no Russians... Four persons spoke only in Russian.[96]

In May 2005, journalist Svetlana Meteleva reported: "Full identification has been established for 17 participants in the attack: one Ukrainian [Khodov], and six Chechens, while the remainder were of Ingush nationality."[97]

The fact that most of the terrorists were Ingush is something that neither the Russian authorities nor the titular head of the terrorists, the Chechen Shamil Basaev, have wanted to admit. The Russian authorities have quite reasonably been leery of re-igniting the incendiary Ossetiyan-Ingush "ethnic Chernobyl," which, in 1992, exploded into heavy fighting in the contested Prigorodnyi

---

95   "Ubitogo boevika Khodova eshche neskol'ko mesyatsev razyskivalo MVD," Ej.ru, 1 September 2005.

96   Pravdabeslana.ru, III, 38.

97   Svetlana Meteleva, "Beslan bez grifov," part II, Mk.ru, 25 May 2005.

District which Beslan borders. That conflict culminated in the ethnic cleansing of some 30,000 Ingush.[98]

As for Shamil Basaev, he, too, seems to have wanted to "chechenize" the terrorist attack, requiring the mostly Ingush terrorists to press for the removal of Russian troops from Chechnya and attempting to scotch their attempts to obtain the release of some 30 mostly Ingush rebels imprisoned for their part in the June 2004 assault on Ingushetiya.[99] Basaev, with the apparent intention of misleading his readers, asserted that the terrorist group at Beslan included twelve Chechen males, two Chechen women, nine Ingush, 2 Arabs, 2 Ossetiyans, and 1 Guran. In writing this, he was seeking to "chechenize" the event. Basaev also denied in his statement that the terrorists had wanted to obtain the release of confederates captured after the June 2004 events in Ingushetiya. "They [the terrorists at Beslan] did not demand that any of the mujehedin be released from prison," he claimed.[100]

One former hostage, Fatima Gutieva, has recalled: "I by myself arrived at the conclusion that they [the terrorist leaders] had switched the task before them [the rank-and-file terrorists]. On the first day they said that they wanted the Ingush rebels to be released... They did not expect that before them would be placed the additional task of obtaining a withdrawal of the troops [from Chechnya]..."[101]

In November 2005, the newspaper *Izvestiya* reported that there may have been three Dagestani Muslims among the terrorists at Beslan and that, if so, all three of them likely escaped. The terrorists were identified by former women hostages—including doctor Larisa Mamitova and policewoman Fatima Dudieva—from photos on a wanted list being circulated by the MVD of

---

[98] On this, see "Eto privedet k bol'shoi krovi," Vremya.ru, 3 September 2004.

[99] See "Zayavlenie Amira Brigady Shakhidov 'Riyadus-Salikh'ina,' Abdallakha Shamilya," Kavkaz-Tsentr, 17 September 2004, republished in chechenpress.info, 17 September 2004, translated into English by BBC Monitoring, published in *Johnson's Russia List*, No. 8372, 17 September 2004.

[100] *Ibid.*

[101] Pravdabeslana.ru, XIX, 25.

Dagestan. Concerning one of those identified, Omar Sheikhulaev, Mamitova recalled that the Russian authorities had informed her "he was an Arab who had been destroyed during the storming [of the school building]."[102]

"The Beasts Came from their Cages"

When the Russian authorities first began to identify the terrorists they had killed during the storm at Beslan, several former high-ranking officers of the Russian secret services who had been elected to the Russian State Duma and were serving on that body's Security Committee expressed outrage. They wondered aloud how it was possible that "there could be persons [among the terrorists] who were supposed at that time to be in places of imprisonment." The deputies sent an official inquiry [zapros] to the MVD, FSB and Russian General Procuracy demanding answers. Among the signatories of these zaprosy were: Vladimir Margelov, a former deputy director for operations of the SVR, Gennadii Gudkov, a former colonel in the FSB, Vladimir Stal'makhov, who had previously worked in the central apparatus of the FSB, and Aleksei Volkov, who had served as the head of the MVD for Kursk oblast'.[103]

A particularly scathing article on the subject of these identifications was published by journalist and Duma deputy Aleksandr Khinshtein. "Both terrible and sensational," he began his article, "is the arithmetic of Beslan: as it turns out, five of the eighteen [identified] terrorists had previously been taken into custody by the special services. They were all caught red-handed, but for some reason…they unfailingly found freedom. Five other participants in the terrorist act were on the wanted list for other crimes, but they [law enforcement] were unable to find them."[104]

---

[102]   "Beslanskikh boevikov uznali sredi zhivykh," Izvestia.ru, 18 November 2005.
[103]   "Duma nachala svoe rassledovanie po Beslanu," Gazeta.ru, 11 September 2004.
[104]   Aleksandr Khinshtein, "Prigovorennye k svobode," Mk.ru, 21 October 2004.

In response to the *zaprosy* submitted by the Duma deputies, both the MVD and the General Procuracy acknowledged that "two of the terrorists had already been brought to trial. One had been freed by the Procuracy 'as a result of a change of circumstance.' The other had been found not guilty by a jury. He was freed a month and a half before Beslan."[105] The terrorist who had been released due to "a change of circumstance" was Khampash [Khan-Pasha, Khan-Pashi] Kulaev, the older brother of the sole terrorist reported by the authorities to have been captured alive at Beslan. A native of the Nozhai-Yurt district of Chechnya, Khampash had been arrested in August 2001 for participating as an active member in a rebel group under the command of field commander Rabani Khalilov.

Khampash lost his arm during an attack by federal aviation. As a result of the amputation of his arm, Khinshtein reported, Khampash had been officially classified as an invalid and, on 16 December 2001, "the criminal case against him was quashed." "What touching, sweet tender-heartedness!" Khinshtein exclaimed, noting that that the one-armed Khampash had been seen by hostages firing a grenade-launcher during the storming of the school by Russian forces.

Another case cited by Khinshtein was that of 23-year-old Isa Torshkhoev. "In June of 1999," Khinshtein recalled, "he [Torshkhoev] carried out a robbery in the home of a family in the Terskii district of Kabardino-Balkariya. The offices of the Mozdok police arrested Torshkhoev while hot on his trail. At the time he was arrested, they found a grenade on him. However in April of 2000 the district court of Mozdok gave him a two-and-a-half year suspended sentence."

"In June of the same year [2000]," Khinshtein continued,

> Torshkhoev was sentenced for a second time—by the Terskii District Court—and this time to two years in prison. But he was amnestied while he was still standing there in the courtroom. The Procuracy did not agree with this decision. After it

---

[105]   *Ibid.*

launched a protest, Torshkhoev fled and was put on the wanted list. They found him only in March of 2001. But when they brought him to Terskii Court, Judge Tolparova (a kindly woman, God grant her health!) immediately released the criminal.

"Torshkhoev's case", Khinshtein added, "was reexamined only in July of 2002... for his having illegally carried a grenade and for robbery... Torshkhoev was then sentenced to four years. Naturally, it was a suspended sentence."

Particularly shocking, in Khinshtein's view, was the case of terrorist Mairbek Shebikhanov.

On the evening of 7 August 2003, on the road between the settlements of Nesterovskaya and Alkhasty, Sunzhenskii District, the group of Shebikhanov fired on an armored transport carrier from ambush. Six soldiers from the Eighth Commandant's company of Groznyi perished, and seven were wounded... On 26 September [2003], together with two other participants in the raid, Shebikhanov was taken into custody in Karabulak [Ingushetiya]. And even though the terrorists put up armed resistance while they were being arrested, on 29 September [2003]—that is, precisely three days later—the procuracy of Karabulak District freed Shebikhanov. The enraged officers of the Ingush UBOP were forced to arrest him again... and take him off to the republic's procuracy.

During the investigation, Khinshtein summed up,

Shebikhanov fully admitted his guilt. He was charged with an entire bouquet of articles from the Criminal Code (murder, terrorism, participation in the NVF [the separatist movement], the illegal possession and bearing of arms). But then something miraculous happened... In July of [2004], the Supreme Court of Ingushetiya found the terrorist not guilty. The verdict was reached by a jury. Shebikhanov left directly from the court and immediately joined the rebels. There were less than two months left until the Beslan tragedy.

Khinshtein also discussed the case of Adam Iliev, a twenty year old Ingush from Malgobek District, who was arrested while caught in the act of making bombs. "A month and a half [after his arrest], an investigator for the Malgobek police for some reason released Iliev on his own recognizance. On the same day, with the agreement of the deputy procurator of the district, the criminal case against him was completely quashed." It was noted by the authorities that Iliev had not been arrested previously and enjoyed good character references. Another "hero" of Beslan discussed by Khinshtein was 27-year-old Chechen Sultan Kamurzoev, who was arrested in February 2000 by the Groznyi department of the MVD for participating in the NVF. Two months later, he was released for time served.

The investigative efforts of Khinshtein and the deputies on the Duma's Security Committee came to naught, and they were soon required to drop the issue. It should be noted that during his trial in the summer of 2005, Nur-Pasha Kulaev confided several times during the proceedings that he and his older brother had de facto been forced by the terrorists to join their band. Both of them, he said, had been accused by the terrorists of "collaboration with the [Russian] authorities." Nur-Pasha maintained at the trial that he "indeed possessed a certification from an employee of the security services of the [pro-Moscow] president of Chechnya."[106] He also said at the trial: "They [the terrorists] came and picked me up because I had prepared documents that I wanted to work with [pro-Moscow deputy Chechen premier] Ramzan Kadyrov."[107]

On the subject of the inexplicable release from prison of certain of the terrorists who later attacked Beslan, former lieutenant colonel in the FSB Aleksandr

---

[106]   "U Kulaeva bylo udostvorenie sotrudnika bezopasnosti prezidenta Chechni," *Nezavisimaya gazeta*, 1 June 2005.

[107]   "Beslanskie terroristy ne khoteli otdavat' Kulaeva Ramzanu Kadyrovu," Lenta.ru, 15 July 2005.

Litvinenko, who had once served as a Russian counter-terrorism specialist, has commented:

> According to the internal orders which regulate the operational secret service activity of the organs of the FSB of the Russian Federation, in the case of persons who have been arrested on suspicion of their participation in illegal armed units...a file of operational work progress is opened... During the work on this case, measures are taken for the operational tracking of the criminal cases and secret measures are taken with regard to the [former] prisoners, i.e., they are shadowed, and, in this connection, they are constantly under the control of the secret services.[108]

Those terrorists released following their arrest by the FSB on terrorism charges, Litvinenko continued,

> could not have left their prisons under any circumstances, without having come into the view of the FSB.... I don't have any doubts that after their detention and arrest... active operational measures were conducted with regard to them and, first of all, measures aimed at turning them into secret collaborators with the FSB. And only after they had been recruited... were they then released to carry out assignments for the special services.

The *Der Spiegel* investigative team drew similar conclusions: "Many of the hostage-takers, especially their leaders, were wanted criminals, some of many years' standing, but they remained unmolested by the police even though they moved about freely in their home village. Other perpetrators had been detained prior to Beslan but were then released for dubious reasons."[109]

---

[108] In Chechenpress.info, 8 September 2004. Translation into English by Norbert Strade. It should be noted that Litvinenko is a close associate of fugitive oligarch Boris Berezovskii.

[109] Buse, Fichtner, Kaiser, Klussmann, Mayr and Neef, "Putins Ground Zero."

Writing in May of 2005, journalist Svetlana Meteleva summed up the situation with regard to these terrorists in the following way:

> The beasts came [to Beslan] from their cages. It was the judges, police and the FSB who opened the cages for them. As for the remaining twelve who have been identified there is no such information [i.e., that they had previously been arrested]. But that is not necessary. It is sufficient to mention that their corpses were identified from fingerprints. That means that each of them was 'on operational registration.'[110]

Allegations of drug addiction among the terrorists also require discussion. In September of 2005, the deputy Russian procurator general Nikolai Shepel' asserted: "No conditions for the freeing of the hostages were put forward [by the terrorists], and none were discussed." He then added contemptuously: "Twenty-seven of the rebels were taking drugs, 22 of them were under the effect of strong narcotics—of heroin and morphine."[111] How, he implied, could one even consider negotiating with drug addicts?

The North Ossetiyan parliamentary commission to investigate Beslan challenged this position of the Russian General Procuracy. In its draft report, the commission concluded, "No traces of strong narcotics were found in the bodies of the rebels, something which coincides with the testimony of the hostages, who underline the high professionalism of the terrorists and are not inclined to consider the rebels banal drug addicts."[112] In similar fashion, doctor Larisa Mamitova has recalled an incident from her captivity at the school: "The Colonel came up to me and said: 'Doctor, do you see any drug addicts here?' I said, 'No.' 'Then,' he said, 'Remember my words, they will call us drug addicts...'"[113]

---

[110]   Meteleva, "Beslan bez grifov," part II.

[111]   "Zamgenprokurora zayavil, chto shturma v Beslane ne bylo."

[112]   Elena Milashina, "Den' neznaniya," *Novaya gazeta*, 1 September 2005.

[113]   Pravdabeslana.ru, VII, 34.

The Terrorists' Demands

Despite Russian deputy procurator general Shepel's heated denial that the Beslan terrorists had wanted to negotiate—President Putin initially made the same claim during his 2 September 2005 meeting with four Beslan Mothers[114]—it seems clear that the terrorists did seek to negotiate with the Russian authorities, albeit with high-ranking and not low-ranking officials. Low-level attempts by the authorities to initiate negotiations were quickly rebuffed by the terrorists: "At 11:00 a.m. [on 1 September], two policemen went up to the building for negotiations, but the terrorists halted them with shots [over their heads]."[115]

According to *Der Spiegel*, one noteworthy attempt by the terrorists to initiate negotiations was effectively jump-started by the North Ossetiyan doctor, Larisa Mamitova, who found herself and her young son numbered among the hostages. Shortly after the school complex had been seized,

> the terrorists addressed the crowd [of hostages] asking for a doctor. Mamitova speaks up. She is led to the main corridor. Two terrorists are sitting there on the floor, leaning against the wall and bleeding profusely. Mamitova figures that one is around 25 years old, the other 35... A bullet has passed through the lower part of the older one's right arm... She bandages the older one first.... Mamitova has the feeling the man is one of the leaders of the hostage-takers. He is particularly aggressive and issues orders to the others...[116]

The two terrorists were wounded during the taking of the school. One of the children's fathers reportedly brought a pistol with him to the school, and he seems to have been able to wound two terrorists and kill another (the deceased rebel's body lay out in the school courtyard until 3 September).

---

114 Natal'ya Galimova, "'My donesli do nego pravdu,'" Mk.ru, 5 September 2005.
115 "Nord-Osetiya," Gzt.ru, 1 September 2004.
116 Buse, Fichtner, Kaiser, Klussmann, Mayr and Neef, "Putins Ground Zero."

"'We have only one goal,' Khodov [the wounded terrorist] said to Mamitova. 'The Russian army must leave Chechnya.' Mamitova suggests that a note with a message be sent outside. 'Only the Colonel can decide that,' Khodov says. 'Then let me talk to the Colonel,' Mamitova says." After some time Mamitova is taken to see the Colonel. "The Colonel seems purposeful and sure, so sure that Mamitova has the feeling he has experience with hostage-taking. The doctor sees that they [the other terrorists] are afraid of the Colonel and they do what he orders."

The *Der Spiegel* account continues:

> The Colonel sits back down at the table with Mamitova. He gives her a sheet of paper and a pen, and dictates a phone number at which the Russian government should call him. Then he digs around in his pants pocket. He pulls out a floor plan of the school, examines it briefly, and puts it back in his pocket. Then he takes out a sheet of paper with writing on it and dictates his demands to Mamitova. The presidents of North Ossetiya and Ingushetiya must come to the school to negotiate, together with Putin's advisor on the Caucasus, Aslambek Aslakhanov, and Leonid Roshal', a Moscow pediatrician and Putin confidant. Twenty hostages will be shot for each wounded hostage-taker, and fifty for each dead one. If the school is stormed, he will blow it up. The Colonel also demands that water be provided from Nazran, Ingushetiya, water, pure water.

Waving a white flag, Mamitova then left the school building to deliver the message. The terrorists told her that they would shoot her son if she attempted to flee. She naturally returned to the building.

In its "Chronicle of the seizure of hostages" posted on 3 September, the website Newsru.com reported at 11:35 a.m. on 1 September that the note carried by Mamitova had been delivered.[117] At 12:10 p.m., the same web-site re-

---

[117]   "Khronika zakhvata zalozhnikov v shkole goroda Beslana v Severnoi Osetii," Newsru.com, 3 September 2004.

ported: "The terrorists who seized the school in Beslan have sent the law enforcement organs a note with a released hostage carrying the text, 'Wait.'"
And at 12:25 p.m. Newsru.com wrote: "The terrorists enter into negotiations
and hand over a video-cassette containing a tape of what had happened inside the school. They also hand over a note in which they demand that the
rebels who attacked Ingushetiya on the night of 22 June be freed."

This final point was confirmed by the website Gzt.ru: "The bandits demanded
that 27 rebels captured after the June raid on Ingushetiya be released from
prison in Vladikavkaz [North Ossetiya], which confirms the version that
Beslan was attacked by a mixed Chechen-Ingush detachment."[118] According
to another former hostage, Ol'ga Vlaskina, "the Colonel" told them: "Your demands [to be transmitted to the Russian authorities] are...to remove the
troops from Chechnya, to halt the war in Chechnya and to release certain of
the rebels who are in prison in Vladikavkaz."[119]

At 2:09 p.m. on 1 September, it was reported: "The terrorists declined to negotiate with Mufti Ruslan Valgosov [of North Ossetiya] and the procurator of
Beslan, Alan Batagov. They did not admit the mufti and the procurator into
the school... In the words of the mufti, the terrorists again declared they
would talk only with Dzasokhov, Zyazikov, and Roshal'."[120] The main telephone negotiator with the terrorists during the first day of the incident was a
rather low-ranking officer of the FSB of North Ossetiya. As Stanislav Kesaev
has noted, "They kept promising him [the local negotiator] that professional
negotiators from Moscow would soon appear. But they did not appear."[121]

The terrorists soon made good on one of their promises. During the first day,
they brazenly executed approximately twenty male hostages inside the
school.[122] Their bodies were later dumped outside the building where they lay

---

[118] "Nord-Osetiya," Gazeta.ru, 1 September 2004.
[119] "Skhvachennogo boevika zalozhniki ne uznayut," Gazeta.ru, 10 September 2004.
[120] "Khronika zakhvata zalozhnikov v shkole goroda Beslana v Severnoi Osetii."
[121] Ol'ga Allenova, "'Byli deistviya, kotorye byli pokhozhi na shturm'," *Kommersant-vlast*, 29 August 2005.
[122] Buse, Fichtner, Kaiser, Klussmann, Mayr and Neef, "Putins Ground Zero."

decomposing. The reasons behind this wanton criminal act have been explained by commentators as being: a desire to get rid of physically strong male hostages who could have caused the terrorists difficulties; a desire to intimidate the other hostages; and, finally, a wish to convince the Russian authorities that their threat to kill the remaining hostages was a credible one.

Seeking to Elicit a Federal Response

There has been some question as to when the name of Aslambek Aslakhanov, President Putin's advisor on the North Caucasus, was added to the list of officials whom the terrorists wanted to come to the school.[123] Doctor Mamitova appears to have forgotten at what point Aslakhanov's name was added to the list. As for the other three names on the list—Zyazikov, Roshal' and Dzasokhov—it seems likely that the terrorists wanted to execute Murat Zyazikov, a former FSB general serving as the president of Ingushetiya, and pediatrician Leonid Roshal', who had been present at Nord-Ost, where he had reportedly collaborated with the Russian secret services. As journalist Sanobar Shermatova has noted: "The rebels repeatedly had tried to kill Zyazikov, and the Ichkeriya web-sites openly call Roshal' an FSB collaborator."[124]

In the case of President Dzasokhov of North Ossetiya and of the Chechen Aslambek Aslakhanov, however, it seems likely that the terrorists wanted them present precisely as negotiators. Dzasokhov had at one point provided (with the knowledge of the Kremlin) refuge to the family of Chechen separatist president Aslan Maskhadov, while Aslakhanov is generally not viewed as close to Putin. During a session in the trial of Nur-Pasha Kulaev, one of the former hostages, Rustam Kokov, recalled: "[Vladimir] Khodov told me that the hostages weren't needed, and he did not intend to kill them. 'We need

---

[123]   On this, see the summary of the draft report of the Torshin commission in Milashina, "Den' neznaniya."

[124]   Sanobar Shermatova, "Peregovory planirovalis'," *Moskovskie novosti*, 5 September 2004.

Dzasokhov [he said]. Your people think that we want to kill him, but we need him alive.'"[125]

As was previously noted, the terrorists released a film cassette on 1 September showing the number of hostages seized. The official Russian response was that the cassette was empty: "They [the terrorists] sent out a cassette in which the demands of the rebels were laid out. But it turned out to be empty."[126] On 7 September, however, the Russian television channel NTV showed a videotape "which was filmed inside the seized school by the terrorists themselves… Judging from everything, the videotape was made on 1 September several hours after the taking of the school… Up until today no-one but the employees of the special services had seen it."[127] So, it turned out, the cassette was not empty after all.

On the morning of the second of September, according to the reconstruction of events carried out by *Der Spiegel*:

> The terrorist at the bomb detonator is sitting in a chair listening to the radio. Larisa Mamitova, the doctor, learns that the government got the message on the slip of paper, but supposedly the phone number does not work. Mamitova asks to speak to 'the Colonel.' She is led to the stairs, and the Colonel comes down from the second floor. The Colonel takes two cell phones and calls one of them with the other. And indeed, the number does not work.

This development then prompted the German reporters to ask: "Has the [Russian] crisis staff in the meantime blocked the number that was working the evening before in order to gain some time? Or to confuse the hostage-takers?"[128]

---

[125] Zaur Farniev, "'Operatsiya po zakhvatu shkoly proshla na vse sto ballov,'" *Kommersant*, 24 June 2005.

[126] Shermatova, "Peregovory planirovalis'."

[127] "Telekanal NTV pokazal videozapis' sdelannuyu terroristom v shkole v Beslane," Newsru.com, 7 September 2004.

[128] Buse, Fichtner, Kaiser, Klussmann, Mayr and Neef, "Putins Ground Zero."

Whatever the case, "The Colonel dictates a new number to Mamitova. She writes the number down on a slip of paper. She also writes that the terrorists are losing their patience." Waving her son's undershirt as a white flag, Mamitova then goes out and delivers the new message. From this point forward, the terrorists were able to cease attempting to take the initiative and to begin to respond to efforts that were being made by moderate political leaders from the North Caucasus (Aleksandr Dzasokhov, Aslambek Aslakahanov, Ruslan Aushev, Mikhail Gutseriev). These negotiations will be covered later on in this report.

President Putin

This study now moves from a consideration of the terrorists' aims to an examination of the negotiation strategy pursued by the Russian president and his subordinates. Putin, who had been vacationing on the Black Sea at the resort town of Sochi, returned by plane to Moscow after learning of the hostage-taking incident. Immediately upon his arrival at the airport in Moscow, he held a meeting with the head of the Russian Ministry of Internal Affairs (MVD), Rashid Nurgaliev, with the Russian Procurator General Vladimir Ustinov, with the director of the FSB, Nikolai Patrushev, and with the first deputy director of the FSB and commander of the Russian Border-guards, Vladimir Pronichev.[129] The presence of General Pronichev at this meeting is of particular significance. Pronichev oversaw the storming of the theater building at Dubrovka in October 2002 in which at least 125 hostages died from the effects of a special gas employed by the FSB.

Following this meeting with his power ministers, Putin placed a call on a secure phone to the elected president of North Ossetiya, former Politburo member (under Gorbachev) Aleksandr Dzasokhov. At approximately noon, Dzasokhov had been conducting a meeting of an ad hoc headquarters that had been formed in an attempt to manage the Beslan crisis. According to an

---

[129] "Boeviki poshli v shkolu," Politcom.ru, 1 September 2004.

eyewitness: "At that time there was a call: the President of Russia gave an [oral] command to hand over the organization of the counter-terrorist operation to the organs of the FSB. There then commenced a complete *bardak* [anarchy]."[130] If this account is accurate, Putin effectively pushed aside the elected president of North Ossetiya, who had de facto assumed command of affairs, replacing him with the leadership of the FSB. As we shall see, this move served to reduce the chances of a negotiated settlement to the crisis.

The next glimpse we have of Putin is on the following day, 2 September. During the televised part of a meeting held in Moscow with King Abdullah II of Jordan, Putin emphasized: "Our chief goal consists, of course, under the situation that has been formed, in saving the lives and preserving the health of those who are hostages. All of the actions of our forces which are concerned with freeing the hostages will be dedicated and subordinated exclusively to that task."[131] Putin then remained out of public view until the morning of 4 September when the storming of the school building had been completed.

Activities of the FSB-Run Headquarters

At noon on 1 September, Putin telephoned the ad hoc headquarters in Beslan being led by President Dzasokhov and verbally ordered that the anti-terrorism operation be put under the command of the FSB. That order is cited in a remarkable document that was leaked to journalist Svetlana Meteleva of *Moskovskii komsomolets*: a 400-page report by an "experts' commission" charged with closely examining the Beslan tragedy. The report, which contained both documents and an analysis, was written by a body chaired by FSB Lieutenant General in the Reserves Ivan Mironov. It also included the deputy head of administration of the "A" Special Purpose Center of the FSB of the Russian Federation, Aleksandr Matovnikov.[132]

---

130 Meteleva, "Beslan bez grifov," part III.
131 "Zayavlenie prezidenta Rossii," Gzt.ru, 2 September 2004.
132 Meteleva, "Beslan bez grifov," parts I-III, Mk.ru, 24-26 May 2005.

Following Putin's oral directive, FSB personnel in Beslan immediately demanded that the MVD take down the "special equipment to scan radio communications" that it had set up. The FSB officers then set up their own equipment. "In sum," observed one MVD officer,

> there existed two headquarters acting in parallel. One, under the leadership of the FSB, concentrated on the operation to free the hostages. But what occurred there and what decisions they adopted—no-one knew. The second [center], the operational headquarters of the MVD, worked on the territory: it set up cordons, evacuated residents, reacted to all announcements. There was no coordination between the two headquarters.[133]

Subsequently Nikolai Patrushev, the director of the FSB, would confirm during a session of the Federation Council—to the dismay of the council's members—that there had been no coordination between the MVD, the FSB, and the army during the hostage-taking.[134] In point of fact, however, as we shall see, the FSB was, when it wanted to, able to impose its will on both the MVD and military in Beslan.

Soldiers of the FSB's Special Purpose Center [spetsnaz] arrived in Beslan during the afternoon of 1 September, and they immediately began coordinating their activities with the FSB-led headquarters. They proceeded to carry out exercises and "to work out their actions in the event of a storm... Not far from Beslan one heard explosions, firing, a village is taken." The spetsnaz were members of two elite FSB counter-terrorist units, "Alfa" and "Vympel," headed up by Colonel General of the FSB Aleksandr Tikhonov, who was appointed the director of the FSB's Special Purpose Center in Moscow in 1998.[135]

---

[133]   Ibid.
[134]   Buse, Fichtner, Kaiser, Klussmann, Mayr and Neef, "Putins Ground Zero."
[135]   "Beslanskaya komissiya zanyalas' spetsnazom," Gazeta.ru, 28 October 2004. See also Buse, Fichtner, Kaiser, Klussmann, Mayr and Neef, "Putins Ground Zero."

A related key development occurred late in the afternoon of the first day of the crisis: "On 1 September, toward evening, at 5:40 p.m., there arrived guests from Moscow—two deputy directors of the FSB, Pronichev and Anisimov." Pronichev, as was previously noted, "had handled the Dubrovka theater siege in Moscow in October 2002."[136] The experts' commission report cited by Svetlana Meteleva confines itself to remarking that these two top-ranking generals issued banal commands such as "Prepare to provide medical assistance to the hostages and the wounded." "But possibly," Meteleva added, "the remaining commands of the generals were so secret that the experts were not told about them. However, immediately following the arrival of Vladimir Pronichev and Vladimir Anisimov at the operational headquarters they remembered about the existence of the press." Henceforth responsibility for all public relations was placed on the heads of the local North Ossetiyan FSB and MVD, Generals Andreev and Dzantiev.[137]

One Potential Negotiator is Physically Removed

A last development relating to the events of 1 September deserves mention. The well-known journalist Anna Politkovskaya, who writes for the pro-democracy newspaper *Novaya gazeta*, was a negotiator who might well have entered into fruitful contact with the terrorists. She had been present at Nord-Ost as a volunteer negotiator and had had certain success there (arguably more than any other negotiator). Politkovskaya decided to fly to Rostov-on-Don and then to travel by car to Beslan. "Finally at about 9:00 p.m. [on 1 September]," she later recalled,

> I succeeded in getting a seat on a plane, ordered a cup of tea, and a certain time later lost consciousness. Already in the hospital [in Rostov] a doctor informed me that I had been poisoned with a powerful unidentified toxic substance. I suspect three FSB officers who were flying in business class... One of

136   Nabi Abdullaev, "Report: Beslan HQ was run by others," *Moscow Times*, 15 April 2005.
137   Meteleva, "Beslan bez grifov," part III, Mk.ru, 26 May 2005.

them addressed the stewardess with a question and the other put a tablet in my cup. I survived by a miracle... I did not conceal that I was going there to initiate negotiations with the terrorists. Honestly speaking, I never thought that they [the special services] would go so far.[138]

In an October 2004 interview, Politkovskaya elaborated on the negotiations she had been intending to conduct with the terrorists in Beslan. On 1 September, according to an article appearing in the British newspaper *The Independent*, Politkovskaya "phoned her rebel contacts and pleaded with them to allow Aslan Maskhadov, former Chechen president and rebel leader, to journey to Beslan and persuade the hostage-takers to release their captives. Having agreed to fly to Beslan and negotiate a safe passage for Maskhadov she set off for the airport." "'My last contact with Maskhadov's people was ten minutes before I got on the plane [she told 'The Independent']. I suppose I did more than a journalist normally does. I then got on the plane and drank some tea and then...nothing.'"[139]

Another potential negotiator, Andrei Babitskii of Radio Free Europe/Radio Liberty, who had visited Chechnya incognito on several occasions, was physically prevented from leaving Moscow. Arriving at the airport from abroad, he was first held by police for allegedly having explosives in his pocket, and was then roughly jostled by "hoodlums" after which he was taken by police to court on a criminal charge.[140] The charge was dropped after the Beslan tragedy concluded. Babitskii was fined and then permitted to return to the West.[141]

---

138 "Anna Politkovskaya: 'Ya vyzhila prosto chudom,'" Rtl.fr, 10 September 2004, Russian translation at Inosmi.ru, 10 September 2004. See also: Anna Politkovskaya, "Poisoned by Putin," *The Guardian*, 9 September 2004.

139 Andrew Osborn, "Anna Politkovskaya: Putin, poison and my struggle for freedom," *The Independent*, 15 October 2004.

140 "V aeroportu 'Vnukovo' militsiei zaderzhan korrespondent Radio Svoboda Andrei Babitskii," Svoboda.org, 2 September 2004.

141 "Babitskomu zamenili arest na shtraf," Grani.ru, 4 September 2004.

Patrushev's Coded Telegram No. 629

On the second day of the crisis, 2 September, a key development occurred in the middle of the afternoon. According to the report of the experts' commission:

> At 2:45 p.m., there came a command from the FSB of the Russian Federation (a coded telegram from Patrushev, number 629, dated 2 September 2004) concerning the naming of the head of the FSB of the Republic of North Ossetiya-Alaniya, Andreev, as the leader of the headquarters. As members of the headquarters were to be included the minister of education of the republic, Levitskaya, the head of the *Zashchita* center, Goncharov, and the deputy director of the information program of 'Rossiya' State Television, Vasil'ev... Now Andreev was the leader on a legal foundation.

While the naming of Andreev was roughly in accord with Russian legislation on terrorism, his appointment ought legally to have come from Prime Minister Mikhail Fradkov, and not from Patrushev. At some point, however, Fradkov reportedly did issue a decree officially naming Andreev head of the operations headquarters.[142]

Russian State Duma deputy Yurii Savel'ev of the *Rodina* faction, who was present in Beslan at the time of the crisis, maintained that FSB Generals Pronichev and Anisimov were there merely "as consultants who had had experience in conducting anti-terrorist operations. In particular, Pronichev had led the operation to free the hostages in 'Nord-Ost' in the fall of 2002."[143] In point of fact, however, the two generals were there not as consultants but in order to run the operation. On 7 September, Savel'ev's colleague in the *Rodina* faction of the State Duma, Mikhail Markelov, who was also present in Beslan throughout the crisis, confided: "I will tell you—the headquarters really worked. It was headed by the first deputy director of the FSB, Vladimir Pro-

---

[142]   Abdullaev, "Report: Beslan HQ was run by others."
[143]   "Nikto ne priznaet otvetsvennosti," *Kommersant-vlast'*, 20 June 2005.

nichev."[144] *Novaya gazeta* Journalist Elena Milashina has drawn similar conclusions: "Patrushev's deputies—Pronichev, Anisimov and others—were in charge of everything at Beslan."[145] A journalist who writes for the government newspaper *Rossiiskaya gazeta*, who was present in Beslan, has recalled General Pronichev's issuing orders at the time of the storming of the school on 3 September.[146]

The Kesaev commission in its draft report has noted that Generals Pronichev and Anisimov, as well as General Tikhonov, the head of the FSB Special Purpose Center, and General Kaloev, the head of the FSB for the Southern Federal District, had all flown in on 1 September. The presence of these very high-ranking FSB officials created a strange situation. "General Andreev was directing his bosses. However, witnesses who were present at the headquarters state that the Moscow FSB leaders and the employees of the Presidential Administration of the Russian Federation created their own parallel headquarters where there was no access for either Andreev or Dzasokhov."[147]

The Kesaev commission goes on to assert:

> The North Ossetiyan commission is convinced that the real leaders of the headquarters were precisely high-ranking personnel of the FSB. The commission evaluates extremely negatively the fact that, in the criminal case, there has been no questioning of the basic participants at the headquarters— General Pronichev, General Anisimov, the leader of the Special Purpose Center Tikhonov, and the head of the FSB of the Russian Federation Patrushev. The commission will insist on the official questioning of the above-named individuals...[148]

---

144   "Protsess byl neupravlayemyi," Gzt.ru, 7 September 2004.
145   Elena Milashina, "Taimuraz Mamsurov," *Novaya gazeta*, 16 June 2005.
146   Timofei Borisov, "Na rasstoyanii pryamogo vystrela," Rg.ru, 7 September 2004.
147   Milashina, "Den' neznaniya."
148   *Ibid.*

Public Relations

One activity the FSB-led headquarters engaged in, a number of sources confirm, was to prepare for an attack on the school building: "The possibility of an assault was being discussed by FSB deputy chief Pronichev and General Tikhonov, the commander of the Alfa and Vympel antiterrorist units...The North Ossetiyan politicians protested vehemently."[149]

The FSB leadership also placed a high priority on public relations activity. General Andreev and other spokesmen at the headquarters attempted heavy-handedly to manufacture a symbolic link between the terrorists who were at the school and the notorious Al-Qaeda. The narrative was carefully crafted.

The web-site Newsru.com reported on 2 September at 11:10 a.m.: "The head of the Moscow bureau of the Qatar television channel Al-Jazeera, Akram Khazam, denied information concerning the channel's alleged intention to act as an intermediary in negotiations with the rebels... [General] Valerii Andreev had announced that the Arab television stations Al-Alam and Al-Jazeera had offered their help in establishing contact with the terrorists." At 2:30 p.m. on the same day, newsru.com reported that a journalist working for the channel Al-Alam "announced that the FSB had approached him with a request to be an intermediary in the negotiations."[150]

Even before the storming of the school building had been completed on 3 September, General Andreev revealed on *Rossiya* State Television that nine of the "destroyed bandits" had been Arabs and that one had been a Muslim "Negro."[151] In an interview with a reporter for *TIME* magazine and other journalists held shortly thereafter, President Putin "blamed the attack [on Beslan]

---

149 Buse, Fichtner, Kaiser, Klussmann, Mayr and Neef, "Putins Ground Zero."

150 "Khronika zakhvata zalozhnikov v shkole goroda Beslana v Severnoi Osetii." General Andreev has confirmed that an approach was made to Al-Alam. See "Protokol doprosa byvshego nachal'nika UFSB RF po RSO-A general-maiora V.A. Andreeva," *Novaya gazeta*, 14 April 2005.

151 "Sredi unichtozhennykh v Beslane terroristov—9 arabov i negr," Newsru.com, 3 September 2004.

on global jihad... He claimed that nine of the hostage takers were from the 'Arab world' and one from Muslim Africa... By linking the terrorists to al-Qaeda, Putin wants to join George W. Bush's global war on terror..."[152]

Another preoccupation of the FSB-led headquarters was to emphasize that there were a mere 354 hostages being held in the school. Aleksandr Torshin, the chair of the Russian parliamentary commission to investigate the Beslan incident, has noted: "The first to cite the figure [of 354 hostages] was Valerii Andreev."[153] This figure—a patently false one—was surfaced by Russian state television and radio early in the morning of 2 September and was being repeated as late as 10:30 a.m. on 3 September.[154]

A representative of one of the Russian power ministries—not the FSB—who wanted to remain anonymous commented to Gazeta.ru: "They [the headquarters] did not cite that figure of 354 right away. If they had, one could accept that they were mistaken. But the figure was cited on the second day... I think that the real figure [more than 1,200] was known to the headquarters. And it was also known to the people in the cordon [around the school]."[155]

The anonymous source continued:

> The first and the main thing is that you have to make it so that the criminals are convinced that there will be no storm [of the building]. And then you prepare for a storm. But in Beslan they did the exact opposite. They convinced the criminals that there would be a storm... The authorities can lie, of course, but the lie must be advantageous for the hostages.... The criminals threw out a cassette as well as a note containing

152   J.F.O. McAllister and Paul Quinn-Judge, "The whole world is crying," TIME Europe, 20 September 2004. According to an RIA novosti press release of 14 October 2004, Russian defense minister Sergei Ivanov claimed at an informal session of the Russia-NATO council held in Romania that "of the 17 identified terrorists who were destroyed in Beslan, five were citizens of Arab states."

153   Valerii Vyzhutovich, "Shmelei ot komissii ne spryachesh'," Moskovskie novosti, 11 February 2005.

154   Buse, Fichtner, Kaiser, Klussmann, Mayr and Neef, "Putins Ground Zero."

155   "V etom shtabe kto khotel, tot i komandoval," Gazeta.ru, 16 September 2004.

demands for the withdrawal of forces from Chechnya and for the arrival of four persons—Dzasokhov, Zyazikov, Aslakhanov and Roshal'.

"But over the [Russian state] television," the source continued,

> the terrorists hear concerning themselves that those who seized the school are strange people who advance no demands, and that no-one knows that they want. But the TV also says that the terrorists are killing the hostages, and the terrorists are listening to that. The first thought in the minds of the terrorists was likely this: the authorities want to prepare public opinion for the fact that we do not agree to negotiations, that we are suicide fighters [*smertniki*], and that in any case the school will be blown up, so something has to be done. The authorities in the final analysis convinced the criminals that there would be a storm, convinced them by their actions.

This analysis is borne out by the testimony of a number of the former hostages. According to one hostage, Albegova, "He [Vladimir Khodov] and the others listened to the news on a radio. He told us that the government claimed that there were 350 hostages. 'They don't need you,' he told us. 'You are expendable. They are lying so that when they storm the building they can cover up the casualties.'"[156] The school principal, Tsalieva, recalled that the leader of the terrorists, the Colonel, "forced her to watch the television news, claiming such misinformation [about 354] hostages] proved that Moscow had written off the hostages."[157]

A number of the former hostages testified that the terrorists "began to act like beasts" after the flagrantly false number of 354 was announced. As a hostage and the mother of a young hostage, Marina Kantemirova, recalled: "On the first day they permitted the children to go to the toilet. But when on television they announced that there were 354 hostages, the terrorists forbade it. They

---

[156] Franchetti and Campbell, "How a repressed village misfit became the butcher of Beslan."

[157] Mark Franchetti, "Beslan turns hate on school director," *Sunday Times*, 17 October 2004.

said: 'We can do anything we want with you, since there are not 1200 of you, but only 354, and the authorities don't need you.'"[158]

The North Ossetiyan parliamentary commission investigating the Beslan incident reached similar conclusions. In its draft report the commission noted: "The responsibility for the intentionally false information concerning the hostages... is borne by the representatives of the federal center: the employee of the Presidential Administration, Dmitrii Peskov, who works for the press secretary of the President of the Russian Federation, [Aleksei] Gromov, and the employee of the Moscow office of Russian State Television, Vasil'ev."[159]

In addition to repeatedly citing a false figure for the number of hostages in the building, the FSB-led headquarters adroitly thwarted the attempts of the terrorists to enter into negotiations. The cell-phone number that the Colonel had dictated to Dr. Mamitova on 1 September was later "blocked." A video-tape made by the terrorists on 1 September was declared "empty," though it was shown over NTV several days later. The authorities dragged their feet in obtaining the release of twenty-seven terrorists captured in June 2004 who could quite realistically have been exchanged for large numbers of hostages, especially young children.

The authorities also sought at one point to bring relatives of the hostage-takers to the school allegedly to put pressure on the rebels. As FSB General Andreev has testified:

> One of the hostages, Kastuev, succeeded in fleeing the school. During his interrogation, he identified from a photograph a resident of the Republic of Ingushetiya, I.I. Kozdoev, from among pictures of those wanted for serious crimes. At the command of....FSB Major General S.B. Koryakov, his family was located—a [former] wife and three children—and they were transported to Beslan. Their appeal to the terrorists

---

[158] "Svyshe 1360 chelovek postradali v Beslane (svidetel'stva ochevidetsev)," Newsru.com, 13 September 2004.

[159] Milashina, "Den' neznaniya."

was recorded on a video-cassette with the aim of using it in the negotiation process. Analogous measures were taken in regard to other participants in the seizure of hostages as information came in concerning the establishment of their identities.[160]

Such measures were bound to irritate, indeed perhaps enrage, the terrorists. Negotiator Ruslan Aushev has recalled: "The commander [i.e., the Colonel] said, you can bring our relatives over here and kill them in the yard. And we will then kill 50% of the hostages."[161]

As military affairs journalist Pavel Felgengauer has rightly concluded, the negotiation techniques of the Russian headquarters served objectively "to drive the terrorists to a frenzy."[162] Was this not, one must ask, their intention all along?

The South Ossetiyan Dimension

If, as some residents of North Ossetiya have argued, the actual aim of the FSB-led headquarters, was to prepare a "coerced storm" of the building, then the significant number of armed South Ossetiyans present in the crowds outside the school would have been seen by them as a potentially useful factor. The president of South Ossetiya, a breakaway region of Georgia, Eduard Kokoity, was present at the headquarters building throughout the crisis.[163] In an interview delivered shortly after the Beslan events, Kokoity noted that he had been a Russian citizen since 1992 and that "98% of the population of our republic are Russian citizens."[164] Among those in the ranks of the *opolchentsy* [homeguard] around the school, *Novaya gazeta* reported at the time, were

---

160 "Protokol doprosa byvshego nachal'nika UFSB RF po RSO-A general-maiora V.A. Andreeva."
161 Seth Mydans, "Negotiator in Russian school hostage case warns revenge could ignite regional violence," *New York Times*, 29 September 2004, p. A8.
162 Pavel Fel'gengauer, "'Shmel'' i 'svin'i'," *Novaya gazeta*, 7 October 2004.
163 Borisov, "Na rasstoyanii pryamogo vystrela."
164 "Yuzhnaya Osetiya—eto uzhe Rossiya," *Nezavisimaya gazeta*, 17 September 2004.

representatives of the "South Ossetiyan MVD."[165] The newspaper *Moskovskii komsomolets* wrote that President Kokoity had brought "reinforcements" with him from South Ossetiya.[166]

A leading human rights web-site, Hro.org, reported on 6 September:

> By the evening of 2 September in the area of the House of Culture there began to gather a group of men in civilian clothing. Several of them were armed. At 10:00 p.m... they put on white gauze armbands. To our question, 'What are those armbands for?' the citizens in camouflage uniforms without epaulettes (judging from their accents, they were of South Ossetiyan origin) answered: 'We are *boeviki* [rebels]. The armbands are so that we will recognize one another.' 'Will you storm the building?' we asked. 'As long as our commander does not say so, we won't.'[167]

Their presence may well have exacerbated the crisis. In early October 2004, *Chechnya Weekly* editor Lawrence Uzzell published a summary of an interview he had conducted with a journalist, Rustam Kaliev, who had been present in Beslan working as a researcher/producer for a Japanese television network. Kaliev told Uzzell, "the gunmen surrounding the school in North Ossetiya included South Ossetiyans—and it was precisely these outsiders who opened fire first on that fatal Friday." Uzzell continued:

> Kaliev said that local residents... who were keeping vigil outside, told him about the South Ossetiyans. They were well armed, he said, with AK-47 assault rifles and high quality sniper rifles... In Kaliev's view, the role of the South Ossetiyans 'was advantageous to the federal authorities—it helped them avoid responsibility.' His theory...is that the South Os-

[165]   Elena Milashina, "O chem govoryat i molchat v Beslane," *Novaya gazeta*, 11 October 2004.

[166]   Aleksandr Khinshtein, "Rab Allakha Basaev...," Mk.ru, 11 October 2004.

[167]   "Beslan: informatsiya pravozashchitnikov," Hro.org, 6 September 2004.

setiyan gunmen were being indirectly manipulated or controlled by the Kremlin.[168]

Vadim Rechkalov, a journalist for the newspaper *Moskovskii komsomolets*, has arrived at similar conclusions: "One can also dump a lot on the *opolchentsy* who were surrounding the school. They [the authorities] say that they were armed and it would have been impossible to drive them away from the cordon. No-one drove them away. Because they, too, were part of the plan."[169]

It has recently come to light that some of these South Ossetiyans present outside the school were recent arrivals in the North, living in the large village of Nogir not far Beslan. "It is believed that southerners [i.e., South Ossetiyans] are more fiery and war-like than northerners... They even began to form up detachments of twenty men near the House of Culture [in Beslan] and collected sign-up lists."[170] After the storming of the building had been completed, *Izvestiya* noted, the Russian secret police cracked down hard on the citizens of Nogir, who were threatening to take active revenge against the Ingush. The role of the armed South Ossetiyans in the storming of the school will be discussed later on in this report.

Moderates from the North Caucasus Seek to Resolve the Crisis

Retired MVD general Aslambek Aslakhanov, who had served in the past as an elected deputy from Chechnya to the Russian State Duma, had been appointed an advisor on the North Caucasus region to President Putin as a kind of consolation prize after he had been forced by the Kremlin to withdraw his candidacy for the post of president of Chechnya in 2003. While being employed as an advisor to Putin, Aslakhanov did not seem to enjoy the Russian president's trust, perhaps because he was seen as too independent a figure.

---

[168] Lawrence A. Uzzell, "A South Ossetian role in Beslan," *Chechnya Weekly*, 6 October 2004.

[169] Vadim Rechkalov, "Tol'ko tak my pobedim vraga...," Mk.ru, 14 September 2005.

[170] Igor' Naidenov, "Beslanskii sindrom," Izvestia.ru, 30 August 2005.

Yet it was his perceived semi-independence that made him an acceptable negotiator to the terrorists holding the hostages in Beslan. As has been noted, Aslakhanov was one of the volunteer negotiators who had come to the theater building at Dubrovka in October 2002 to conduct talks with the terrorists ensconced there.

In an interview with the BBC's Channel 4 news, Aslakhanov, who recalled that he "was on the phone to the hostage-takers within hours of their seizing the school," was asked why fifty-four hours were allowed to elapse before he was able to arrive in Beslan. "Aslakhanov's own explanation," the BBC noted, "is confused. Even though he was Vladimir Putin's man, there was apparent reluctance to vest in him the presidential authority needed—perhaps because of Putin's personal reluctance to even engage with those responsible..." "Aslakhanov said: 'I reported my conversations with the hostage-takers to my boss, who's in charge of the President's office. I told him I thought I should fly down there immediately to start the process of negotiating and initiate contact. I was told that until they [the terrorists] announced their demands and conditions, there wasn't any point in my going.'"[171]

"I had two conversations [with the terrorists] on 1 September," Aslakhanov went on to recall, "I discovered that they had taken not 350 or 400 people, as was being reported, but as he [the Colonel] said, more than 1,200 hostages, over 70 percent of whom were children. I reported this to the media on the first day." The BBC then commented: "But, strangely, it's not what the media was reporting. Aslambek Aslakhanov's information did not get through."

In mid-September 2004, at a press conference in Moscow, Aslakhanov elaborated on what he had discussed with the terrorists:

> Aslakhanov said that they [the terrorists] were demanding a complete withdrawal of Russian troops from Chechnya, recognition of Chechen independence and the release of those

---

[171]   Jonathan Miller, "Putin knew more," Channel4.com, 13 October 2004. URL: http://channel4.com/news/2004/10/week_beslan.html

arrested in connection with the attacks in Ingushetiya. They said they would execute fifteen children every hour if the troops were not withdrawn within two days. And I told them, 'Look, you are putting forth unthinkable conditions. Do you realize what a withdrawal of troops really means? It is a huge military machine. It would take several months.'[172]

On the occasion of the first anniversary of the terrorist incident, in September 2005, Aslakhanov told journalists:

The Russian authorities were prepared to exchange the hostages in School No. 1 in Beslan for those earlier taken into custody on a charge of participating in the attack on Ingushetiya in June 2004... He had three telephone conversations with the terrorists who were holding the children ... 'The third time I succeeded in reaching the terrorists on 2 September in the evening, at 7:00 p.m. I said to them: 'You have declared that you want to have your confederates released who were arrested for the attack on Ingushetiya. We are prepared to discuss that. Only we have to decide how many children you are prepared to release for each rebel. Ten? Twenty? We have something to talk about.' They answered me, 'Good, we will await you at 3:00 p.m.' I asked: may I come in the morning? He [presumably the Colonel] said, no, come at 3:00 p.m., and we will begin our negotiations. They [the Russian authorities] gave me a government plane, and I flew to Beslan, but I had only arrived there, come to the airport, when one explosion sounded, then a second.[173]

A Beslan resident testified at the trial of Nur-Pasha Kulaev, however, that she had seen Aslakhanov in the town at 11:30 a.m. on 3 September.[174] If accurate, this report suggests that Aslakhanov arrived somewhat earlier than he has indicated.

---

[172] Kim Murphy, "Critics detail missteps in the school crisis," *Los Angeles Times*, 17 September 2005.

[173] "Aslakhanov rasskazal o chem dogovorilsya s terroristami v Beslane," Newsru.com, 9 September 2005.

[174] Pravdabeslana.ru, VI, 39.

Independent reports appear generally to confirm Aslakhanov's narrative. In mid-September 2004, it was reported:

> [Police] operatives have told *Kommersant* that the authorities were in principle ready to agree to the demand of the terrorists that those who had been taken into custody for the attack on Ingushetiya on 22 June be freed. The terrorists were speaking about 30 detained persons, but in the Vladikavkaz jail there were only eight of them. And one of that number flatly refused to be freed and to go to his brothers in arms. They succeeded in convincing him only on 3 September.[175]

If accurate, this report appears to be evidence of significant foot-dragging by the Russian authorities. The release of the 27-30 terrorists held in Russian jails constituted a useful bargaining chip that could conceivably have led to the release of many of the children.

The Role of Former Ingush Leaders Mikhail Gutseriev and Ruslan Aushev

Mikhail Gutseriev, an ethnic Ingush who had in the past served as a deputy speaker of the Russian State Duma and was at that time the president of the large *Rusneft'* oil company, arrived in Beslan either late in the day on 1 September or very early on 2 September. Shortly after his arrival, Gutseriev called the terrorists on his mobile telephone. In his discussions with an individual who called himself "Sheikhu" (presumably the Colonel), Gutseriev reportedly asked, "What are your conditions?" "We will hand them over in writing?" he was told. "To whom?" he asked. "To Aushev?" "Aushev?," Sheikhu replied, "Let him come. We guarantee him his life."[176]

---

[175] "Beslan: Boeviki shli na delo sem'yami." See also, Mariya Martova, "Uslovie No 1: Boeviki trebuyut osvobodit' militsionerov, rasstrelyavshikh Ingushetiyu," Mk.ru, 3 September 2004.

[176] Khinshtein, "Rab Allakha Basaev...."

Ruslan Aushev then flew to Beslan. He recalls:

> I was telephoned by one of the leaders of the FSB and by
> Sergei Shoigu [the Russian minister for emergency situations].
> When we arrived on 2 September, Mikhail Gutseriev was
> there with his brother Khamzat, the former minister of internal
> affairs of Ingushetiya. And they were already talking to the ter-
> rorists on the phone... We connected with the terrorists
> through their 'press secretary' [possibly Khodov], and I told
> him that I am Aushev, Ruslan, and he promised to report it to
> the Emir. Then they called back, and they said I could
> come.[177]

In their account of this episode, the authors of the *Der Spiegel* report noted:
"Like the Gutseriev brothers who had been alerted out of sheer desperation,
Aushev is a man whom Putin dislikes intensely. Like them, he too is not allowed into the crisis staff building where Putin's envoys are meeting. From
then on Aushev does his phoning and organizing from the yard outside."[178]

Before proceeding to the school, Aushev performed a favor for President
Dzasokhov of North Ossetiya:

> Ruslan Aushev...uses his cell phone to call his old comrade
> [Chechen separatist spokesperson] Akhmed Zakaev in Lon-
> don.... It is only with the second attempt that a connection is
> made. Aushev hands the phone over to North Ossetiyan
> President Dzasokhov, who, in 1999, when the second
> Chechnya war broke out, offered Maskhadov's wife and
> daughter refuge in his republic. They know each other, re-
> spect each other, and owe each other... Zakaev promises to
> contact Maskhadov and ask him to help. Dzasokhov then
> calls Putin again. The Russian president is willing to negoti-
> ate the release of imprisoned terrorists if, in exchange, a
> 'large number' of children are released from the gymna-
> sium.[179]

---

[177] Fedor Chekhoev, "Pochemu zagovoril Aushev," Strana.ru, 28 September 2004.
[178] Buse, Fichtner, Kaiser, Klussmann, Mayr and Neef, "Putins Ground Zero."
[179] *Ibid.*

In the protocol of Aushev's official questioning on 14 September, one reads:

> At about 2:00 p.m., on 2 September 2004, I [Aushev] went by myself to School No. 1... In the courtyard of the school I was met by rebels in masks who brought me into the school building... A certain time later there entered a man [the Colonel] who seemed to be about thirty, without a mask, with a fluffy beard, without a moustache, with large features on his face. I asked what he was called and he said, 'Call me Rasul.' This man declared that the detachment had come to Beslan on the orders of Shamil Basaev. I asked him to show me the hostages in the gymnasium. Rasul permitted it, and, accompanied by Rasul and two rebels, I went into the gymnasium.[180]

According to a report published by journalist Sanobar Shermatova on 5 September: "In the description of eyewitnesses [i.e., former hostages], the rebels brought [Aushev] into the gymnasium, and one of them began to film on a video-camera the hostages, over whose heads on a wire there hung plastic bottles containing explosives. Having finished this work, the cameraman handed the video-cassette to Aushev. In the opinion of the hostages, to transmit to Putin."[181] On this cassette, it has been reported, "are hundreds and hundreds of living people. And not '200-300 persons.' State Radio and Television [later] declared the tape to be empty."[182] A copy of this "empty" tape was later acquired by CBS Television.

While in the school, Aushev convinced the terrorists to release a small number of hostages. "Passing by one of the rooms," he later recalled, "I saw nursing children and asked the head of the rebels: 'Let the nursing children out,' and he agreed. One of the small children was carried by an older girl. The Emir did not let the girl out, and I took the child out in my arms."[183] Aushev

---

180   Meteleva, "Beslan bez grifov," part II, Mk.ru, 25 May 2005.

181   Sanobar Shermatova, "Peregovory planirovalis'," *Moskovskie novosti*, 5 September 2005.

182   Dmitrii Muratov, "Odin," *Novaya gazeta*, 14 October 2004.

183   Andrei Riskin, "Goryachie golovy gotovy razygrat' ingushskuyu kartu," *Nezavismaya gazeta*, 29 September 2004.

added: "The Emir took the decision [to release the mothers and nursing children] independently—he didn't call anyone."[184]

While he was in the school, Aushev was also given a copy of the demands of the terrorists written down on a sheet torn from a student notebook. Aushev remembers:

> The text began with the words, 'To His Excellency President Putin' and it was signed 'From the slave of Allah, Shamil Basaev.' I was forced to read what was written aloud, and I remember well its demands: stop the war; withdraw the forces; Chechnya enters into the CIS but remains in the ruble zone; in addition, Chechnya, together with the federal forces, introduces order in the North Caucasus and does not permit any third force there. The decree of the president of Russia concerning a withdrawal of forces must be read on television.[185]

Aushev concluded: "One of the rebels then added to the sheet of paper that for each killed rebel 50 hostages would be executed and for each wounded one—20. They also added [in writing] that with the appearance of a decree on the withdrawal of troops they would begin to release the hostages."[186]

To date, the Russian authorities have not made public the text of this list of demands from Basaev. On 17 September, however, Basaev posted what appeared to be its text on the Kavkaz-Tsentr website.[187] Its demands are the same as those that were summarized by Aushev. This appears to confirm that the Russian leadership was aware of the terrorists' terms.

Aushev also offered some personal impressions of the mind-set of the terrorists: "In the words of Aushev, the terrorists planned to conceal themselves after committing the terrorist act, shielding themselves with the hostages. The

---

[184] "Aushev: terroristy rashchityvali uiti iz Beslana," Grani.ru, 10 October 2004.
[185] Riskin, "Goryachie golovy gotovy razygrat' ingushskuyu kartu."
[186] "Aushev: terroristy rasschityvali uiti iz Beslana."
[187] "Zayavlenie Amira Brigady Shakhidov 'Riyadus-Salih'iina' Abdallakhiya Shamilya."

rebels did not want to die and, probably, hoped that the situation would de-velop as it had at the time of the seizure of the hospital in Budennovsk in 1995, when detachments of the extremists succeeded in escaping." And Aushev added: "The rebels always said that we should conduct negotiations with Maskhadov, as even the radical part [of the separatists] consider Mask-hadov to be their president."[188]

Once he had exited from the school, Aushev handed over the sheet of paper containing the rebels' demands to FSB General Valerii Andreev, who trans-mitted it to Moscow. It is not said to whom he gave the video-cassette (later declared to be empty).

> According to Ruslan Aushev, everyone hoped that the advisor
> to the president on questions of the North Caucasus, Aslam-
> bek Aslakhanov, would bring from the capital an answer to the
> ultimatum so that there should be something to talk about with
> the rebels. All the more so since by that time the headquarters
> had connected with Akhmed Zakaev...and on one of the sites
> of the separatists there had been placed a letter by Aslan
> Maskhadov condemning the terrorist act.[189]

Aushev recalled several days after the Beslan events that he had been ex-pecting to go to the school on 3 September together with Aslakhanov. He in-tended to bring with him the "very good statement" that had been posted by Maskhadov on the Internet. "I wanted to show them [the terrorists]: This is what Maskhadov says. What do you need further? Free them [the hos-tages]."[190]

A final agreement reached by Aushev with the terrorists was that several em-ployees of the Ministry for Emergency Situations were to be permitted to come to the school on 3 September to pick up the twenty-one bodies of exe-

---

[188] "Aushev rasskazal podrobnosti peregovorov s terroristami, zakhvativshimi shkolu v Beslane," Newsru.com, 28 September 2004.

[189] Riskin, "Goryachie golovy gotovy razygrat' ingushskuyu kartu."

[190] Dmitrii Muratov, "My poteryali poltora dnya," Novaya gazeta, 6 September 2004.

cuted men that had been thrown outside the school and were decomposing badly.

Although Aushev's role in gaining the release of 26 hostages and in furthering the negotiation process were appreciated by some commentators in Russia, others criticized him sharply for suspected collusion with the rebels. For example, Duma deputy Yurii Savel'ev, who was present in Beslan, asked pointedly: "Why did the rebels release Aushev from the school when they had invited three people there with the goal of killing them?"[191] "They are trying to hang Beslan on Aushev," noted journalist Natal'ya Gevorkyan, "because those who seized the school did not kill him. Is this normal logic?"[192]

On 12 September, a Russian nationalist newspaper, Zhizn', reported that a relative and former bodyguard of Ruslan Aushev named Magomed Aushev had been among the terrorists killed in the storming of the school building. The German newspaper Focus looked into this question. On 27 September it concluded that that the "[Russian] special services" had indeed reported that Magomed Aushev had been killed in the school building but that in fact "Magomed Aushev is living peacefully in Ingushetiya."[193] In an interview with Kavkazskii uzel Magomed Aushev affirmed that he was very much "alive and healthy" and living in Ingushetiya.[194] This incident seemed to indicate an effort by elements in the special services directly to link Ruslan Aushev to the terrorists.

President Putin's personal view of Ruslan Aushev emerged during his discussion with four Beslan Mothers in Moscow on 2 September 2005. Putin stated: "The best specialists did everything possible to save the hostages. But the terrorists did not agree to negotiations." The perplexed Mothers then re-

---

[191] Muratov, "Odin."

[192] Natal'ya Gevorkyan, "Beslanskaya trenirovka," Gazeta.ru, 14 October 2004.

[193] Maksim Artemov, "Beslanskii terrorist voskres iz mertvykh," Utro.ru, 27 September 2004.

[194] "Rodstvennika Ruslana Ausheva 'pokhoronili' vmeste s beslanskimi terroristami," Polit.ru, 22 September 2004. See too the article on Magomed Aushev: "'Ya ne zakhvatyval Beslan!'," Mk.ru, 28 May 2005.

sponded: "What do you mean? Why then did they let Aushev into the school, and why did the terrorists communicate with Gutseriev on the telephone?" To which Putin answered: "All of that was done in stages. At first the terrorists indeed did not agree to negotiations, but then they did. For them Aushev is one of their own [*svoi*], an authority; therefore they agreed to let him in."[195]

In a path-breaking series of articles entitled, "Beslan without signature stamps," journalist Svetlana Meteleva related confidential information obtained from an employee of the Russian special services who had been an eyewitness to events in Beslan: "Keep in mind, no-one will confirm this," he told her,

> But everyone who was at the headquarters and had any relation to the negotiations knows. From the very beginning, the rebels were offered money and a 'green corridor.' They designated a figure for negotiations—Maskhadov. They made contact with Maskhadov through Zakaev. Those two were to appear in Beslan under a guarantee of immunity and to take away the terrorists with them. An agreement was achieved....
> *You want to say* [Meteleva asked] *that the rebels agreed to leave?*
> Yes.
> The question concerned the Budennovsk variant. On the night from the third to the fourth Maskhadov and, possibly, Zakaev were to appear. The terrorists would release a majority of the hostages—in the first place, children. With the remaining hostages they would get in vehicles and leave across the border, into Georgia. There they would release the people. Of course, everything was far from immediately resolved, but it was resolved. The vehicles were ready for them...[196]

Both Maskhadov and Zakaev were willing to come to Beslan to negotiate for the hostages' release. Maskhadov confirmed his intentions prior to his assas-

---

195 Natal'ya Galimova, "'My donesli do nego pravdu'," Mk.ru, 5 September 2005.
196 Meteleva, "Beslan bez grifov," part I, Mk.ru, 24 May 2005.

sination on 8 March 2005, a fact also verified by his son, Anzor.[197] On 3 September 2004, Zakaev noted:

> I said [to Aushev and Dzasokhov] that, as far as the question concerns me, I am prepared immediately to come to Beslan and do what I can in negotiations with the group that had seized the school... However, only the participation in the negotiations—through his representative or personally—of Aslan Maskhadov can resolve this crisis. I assured Dzasokhov and Aushev that Aslan Maskhadov takes to heart the fate of the children no less than they do and that he will come to the place of the tragedy if the Russian side can guarantee him his security...[198]

The Storm Begins

At 3:20 p.m. on 2 September, the commander of the FSB Special Purpose Center, General Tikhonov, "asked the 58th army to send in tanks and armored personnel carriers."[199] These tanks and APCs then came under the direct control of the FSB. Journalist Elena Milashina subsequently reported:

> We observed the preparation for the storm on 2 September. Practically all residents were removed from the multi-floor houses closest to the school. On the roofs, with short rushes, there moved about our *spetsnaz*. Professional School No. 48 (located not far from the school) was transformed into a headquarters, where our special services and the soldiers from the 58th army took up residence.... Into Beslan there arrived prac-

---

[197] See "Maskhadov gotov byl pozhertvovat' soboi radi spaseniya detei," Chechenpress.com, 21 September 2004; Efim Barban, "Maskhadov sobiralsya v Beslan," *Moskovskie novosti: spetsvypusk*, 6 September 2004; Aburashid Saidov, "Chto predlagaet Maskhadov," *Novaya gazeta*, 28 October 2004 (interview with Anzor Maskhadov).

[198] "Dobryi znak," Chechenpress.com, 3 September 2004. On the assassination of Maskhadov, see Anna Politkovskaya, "Taina unichtozheniya Maskhadova," *Novaya gazeta*, 19 September 2005.

[199] Buse, Fichtner, Kaiser, Klussmann, Mayr and Neef, "Putins Ground Zero."

tically all the forces needed for an attack—Alfa, Vympel, the
GRU *spetsnaz*, OMON, SOBR etc.[200]

Shortly before 1:00 p.m. on 3 September, four employees of the Ministry for
Emergency Situations slowly drove up to the school in order to collect the
bodies of the 21 murdered hostages lying in the courtyard. "One of the terrorists came out and demanded that they bring inside [the school] the body of a
confederate who was also lying in the courtyard. They did so, and when they
came out, an explosion and shots rang out."[201]

Doctor Larisa Mamitova later recalled:

> He [the Colonel] said to me, 'There are 21 bodies… Now the
> Ministry for Emergency Situations will come up and collect the
> bodies. You should speak through the window with the Minis-
> try for Emergency Situations. Tell them about the condition of
> the children.' They wanted in every way possible for the peo-
> ple outside to know about the condition of the children. 'I said
> fine.'… [Mamitova then asked:] 'When is the Ministry for
> Emergency Situations coming, what did they say?' They an-
> swered: 'They said it would be in five minutes. Go back to the
> hall. When they arrive, we'll call you.'… They were all calm.
> For some reason it seemed to me that precisely with the arri-
> val of the Ministry for Emergency Situations everything began.
> The shooting began from out there, from out there the storm
> began.[202]

In September 2005, journalist Vadim Rechkalov revealed that he had been
able to interview one of the four rescuers from the Ministry for Emergency
Situations:

---

[200]   Elena Milashina, "Lozh' provotsirovala agressiyu terroristov," *Novaya gazeta*, 6
September 2004. OMON and SOBR are elite forces of the Ministry of Internal Affairs.

[201]   "Doktor Roshal'," Strana.ru, 8 September 2004.

[202]   Pravdabeslana.ru, VII, 29, 35.

On the same day, 3 September [2004], I succeeded in talking with one of the rescuers who survived [two had been shot dead by the terrorists]. He, wounded in an arm, which was bandaged, stood and wept.... I am not naming this person at his request: 'I had a direct telephone connection with their leader [the Colonel],' the officer told me at that time. 'He [the Colonel] warned: 'Let there be no freaks among you.' We came up in the truck, opened the doors, opened the side panels, showed that they were empty, carried a corpse of a rebel onto the porch since they themselves were afraid to take it from an exposed place. Then the doctor went with them around the corner, and we remained standing at the fence with our hands up. And here there began shooting. There had been no explosion before this. After someone opened fire, the rebels began to shoot at us. If no-one had shot, then everything would have been normal. We were absolutely certain that we would return safely.'[203]

And Rechkalov continued:

If one supposes that the authorities planned the storm in advance, then the visit of the rescuers was one of the points in that plan. A vehicle of the Ministry for Emergency Situations enters the territory of the school. A part of the rebels are required to be distracted by that vehicle. To check it out to make sure that under the guise of rescuers the *spetsnaz* did not penetrate into the school. The rebels were not expecting a storm during those moments. At the least, because in their hands there were four Ministry for Emergency Situations personnel. And it was precisely in those minutes that the storm began. And the rescuer said correctly that it was a set-up. Some federals, for the sake of an effect of suddenness, set up other federals—employees of the Ministry for Emergency Situations. And moreover, the rescuer stated that first there was shooting and only then explosions... That is, the battle did not begin with an explosion, as the official version goes, but with the shooting.[204]

---

[203] Mk.ru, 14 September 2005.
[204] *Ibid.*

At approximately 1:00 p.m. on 3 September, all hell quite literally broke loose at School No. 1 in Beslan. According to a chronology of events compiled by the web-site Gzt.ru: "At 1:01 p.m. there resounds the first explosion. Four minutes later—the second. Twenty minutes later—the third... At 1:30 p.m., the roof collapses and there begins a strong fire."[205] At 1:10 p.m., FSB Major General Andreev, the nominal leader of the attacking Russian force, ordered an armed assault on the school building.[206]

There exists, as we have seen, a major difference of opinion between the Russian Procuracy, on the one hand, and both the Kesaev Commission and the Beslan Mothers, on the other, concerning what caused the explosions, the fire, and the collapse of the roof of the gymnasium. These differences merit closer examination. In its draft report, the Kesaev commission con-cluded:

> The first explosions unquestionably had a behind-the- scenes dimension, both a legal and a political one. The possible ap-pearance in Beslan of Maskhadov and Zakaev placed the Kremlin before a complex choice: to permit the saving of the hostages and thus to legalize the figure of Maskhadov and to permit the possibility of a political regulation of the Chechen problem. An unprepared storm, as a variant of the develop-ment of events, by contrast, allowed such a situation not to be permitted.[207]

A resident of Beslan, El'brus Nogaev, pointedly asked deputy Russian procu-rator general Vladimir Kolesnikov in September 2005:

> Why did the explosion take place precisely when agreement had been reached with Maskhadov? That he was to come— that is contained in the testimony of Dzasokhov. He [Dzasok-hov] convinced [the residents of Beslan] that new people were

---

205   "Tri dnya v Beslane," Gzt.ru, 31 August 2005.
206   "Zamgenprokurora zayavil, chto shturma v Beslane ne bylo."
207   Milashina, "Den' neznaniya."

to come, in two hours... In the newspaper I read the testimony of Dzasokhov that he had come to agreement with Maskhadov through Zakaev, and he announced at the Palace of Culture that Maskhadov was coming. And an hour later there occurred the first explosion... Was that really accidental?

Kolesnikov responded, "I don't know... We'll check it out..."[208] At the trial of terrorist Nur-Pasha Kulaev, the accused visibly angered Russian procurators by remembering aloud that, directly after the first explosion occurred, the Colonel had shouted to his confederates that a Russian sniper had killed the terrorist whose foot was on a pedal controlling a powerful bomb. Despite repeated hostile questioning by the procurators, Kulaev stuck stubbornly to his story. Russian deputy procurator general Nikolai Shepel' insisted, in sharp contrast, that, "the examination has shown that snipers present around the school could not have shot the rebel who was controlling the button [pedal], inasmuch as he was located behind plastic, non-transparent windows, and the sniper could not have seen him."[209]

At one point, one of the procurators addressed Kulaev sarcastically:

> *How could a sniper, through windows that were screened with plastic, see the rebel standing on the button and kill him?*
> [Kulaev responded:] It [the plastic] wasn't there. They removed it so that the people could breathe. They took away the plastic... The Colonel said that a sniper shot him from the roof, from a five-story building.
> *But you didn't see it?*
> I know that they removed plastic from the windows.[210]

Kulaev's statements seemed to be supported by testimony from former hostages:

---

208   "Vladimir Kolesnikov," *Novaya gazeta*, 12 September 2005.

209   "Zamprokurora zayavil, chto shturma v Beslane ne bylo." The large windows in the gymnasium were reported to be "two stories tall." Baker and Glasser, *Kremlin Rising*, 16.

210   Pravdabeslana.ru, III, 35.

On the first day, the older students [acting under orders from the terrorists] smashed out the windows with something wooden. The glass was smashed out on the upper parts of the windows from the side of the courtyard. Then, on the second day, they smashed out all the windows completely... In the middle [of the gymnasium] a terrorist was sitting on a chair. He called over another rebel and showed him something in the window. The other one looked over there, and they then forced men [i.e., hostages] to crawl up there, and they hung up a black curtain.
How many windows were smashed out?
From the right side only the upper [parts of the] windows. And from the other side they smashed one out, and then they saw something and hung up a curtain.[211]

Journalist Svetlana Meteleva was able to interview an expert on explosives who had examined the evidence at Beslan:

[Meteleva:] *If one proposes that the reason for the explosion was the death of the operator, could he have been 'removed' by a shot from our [Russian] sniper?*
In the protocol it is said clearly: the operator put into action the explosive chain either through carelessness or because he was wounded or killed. Therefore, yes, our sniper could have shot the terrorist.[212]

During Putin's meeting with four Beslan Mothers on 2 September 2005, the issue of a possible Russian sniper surfaced: "Putin [the Mothers reported] said that there is an eyewitness who saw how a rebel was reading the Koran and then he took his foot [off the pedal] and an explosion sounded. But we told him there was no such testimony at the trial... 'That means [Putin then said] that I have incorrect information. I will have it checked.'"[213]

---

[211]   *Ibid.*, VI, 35.
[212]   Meteleva, "Beslan bez grifov," part I, 24 May 2005.
[213]   Galimova, "My donesli do nego pravdu."

As it turns out, however, both the Mothers and President Putin were in error in their statements on this question. During the Kulaev trial, former hostage Madina Sasieva-Salbieva was asked by a procurator:

> *Were you watching closely the rebel at the controls?*
> Yes.
> *What were his actions before the explosion?*
> When he was reading the Koran or what he did after?...
> *Well, when he was reading what did he do?*
> He just stayed there, and he was killed.
> *Did he take his foot off the controls when he finished reading?*
> I did not notice.
> *Are you giving the same testimony today that you gave in the preliminary investigation? As regards that rebel?... You said then that he finished reading the Koran, put it aside, and then took his foot off the controls.*
> Well, I did not notice that he took his foot away....
> *There in the records it is written that he was reading the Koran and took away his foot.*
> I didn't say that.
> *How are we to understand that? You mean, they wrote it down incorrectly? Didn't you read what the investigator wrote down!!!*
> I read it.
> *I have no further questions.*[214]

What seems to have happened here is that the former woman hostage had been pressured by investigators into giving false testimony concerning the terrorist at the pedal but had then bravely repudiated it at the open forum of the trial. Presumably President Putin was not informed about her change of testimony.

One other hostage, Zarina Tokaeva, claimed to have been watching the rebel manning the pedal at the moment that he was shot:

---

[214] Pravdabeslana.ru, XIX, 33-35.

> When the [first] explosion occurred I well remember the sound
> of tape coming unstuck....My head was turned toward the re-
> bel who sat on the button. When the tape came unstuck, I
> paid attention that he...without writhing fell over on his left
> side. After that the explosion sounded.
> *That is, he lost consciousness?*
> I don't know what was with him, but when people lose con-
> sciousness they go limp. But he was just sitting there and then
> he fell over on his side.[215]

At the trial of Nur-Pasha Kulaev, Beslan policewoman Fatima Dudieva testified that, growing stiff from lack of physical activity, she had stretched her arm
up above one of the window sills in the gymnasium as a form of exercise and
"At that moment it was if someone had thrown a stone through the window.
There was a wild shot of some kind. I sensed that the shot had come from
outside [the school]...I noticed that blood was flowing from my hand and that
my hand was spinning about. I sensed that the glass [in the window] was fly-
ing and I heard the sound of [broken] glass." The first explosion then
sounded. "The second explosion came not immediately but two minutes
later."[216]

There is also possible evidence regarding the second explosion. Journalist
Vadim Rechkalov of *Moskovskii komsomolets* has recalled a conversation
from the day following the storm:

> I walked around the courtyard of the Beslan school together
> with an acquaintance, an employee of the central apparatus of
> the FSB, on the afternoon of 4 September 2004. The corpses
> of the rebels still lay there in a row. The [deceased] children
> had already been carried away. We went up to the frame of
> the gymnasium. Under the right lower window there yawned a
> hole 80 centimeters in diameter. The wall, with a thickness of
> forty centimeters, had been pierced through. I asked my com-

---

[215]   *Ibid.*, XVIII, 13.

[216]   *Ibid.*, XIII, 35. See also the account of Dudieva's statement at the trial in "'Gde te
troe, kogo poimali vmeste s Kulaevym,'" Gazeta.ru, 12 July 2005. Dudieva stated
that one of her fingers had been nicked by a heavy bullet.

panion how that opening had been formed. This is what he answered at the time: 'Our explosive specialists blew out the wall after the beginning of the storm. They did it with a directed explosion. They made a hole so that it would be easier for the children to run out.'[217]

"At that time," Rechkalov recalls,

> I did not ascribe any importance to his words. But in Moscow it had already dawned on them that that explosion was one of the indirect proofs that the rebels in the gymnasium had not blown anything up, that on 3 September 2004 at 1:05 p.m., the storm [of the building] had begun. And the blowing out of [a section of] the wall of the gymnasium represented the beginning of the storm.[218]

At the moment when the first explosion and initial gunfire sounded, negotiator Mikhail Gutseriev and the Colonel were engrossed in negotiations concerning the imminent arrival of Aslakhanov and Aushev at the school. Both were reportedly taken by complete surprise: "'What have you done?!' screamed Gutseriev into the receiver. 'You deceived us,' roared 'Sheikhu' [the Colonel] in response. 'Now you will bear responsibility for everything.' "There is no storm,' Gutseriev tried to calm him. However the situation went out of control."[219] Seeing children escaping from the school, the volunteer *opolchentsy* who were positioned close to the building rushed in to rescue the children. A number of them, as has been noted, were armed South Ossetiyans; in addition to saving children they intended to kill terrorists. The storm had begun.

---

[217] Rechkalov, "Tol'ko tak my pobedim vraga...."
[218] *Ibid.*
[219] Khinshtein, "Rab Allakha Basaev ego prevoskhoditel'stvu Putinu...."

The Gymnasium Roof Burns and Collapses

There has been heated discussion of why the school gymnasium's roof began to burn. In the course of a late June 2005 interview given to the web-site Vremya.ru, Stanislav Kesaev, the head of the North Ossetiyan parliamentary commission to investigate Beslan, remarked:

> There is the testimony of the [Russian military] sapper who, after the first two explosions, broke into the building [the gymnasium] and disconnected the chain [of explosives]. The fire there was small, and we have testimony that fire-extinguishers could easily have put it out.
> *That is, the sappers who broke into the building after the first two explosions disconnected the chain [of explosives], and those bombs could not then be detonated?*
> Yes, they could not be detonated. But the third explosion occurred 20-25 minutes later. That is when everything began.[220]

Former hostage Marina Karkuzashvili-Miskova provided corroborating testimony for Kesaev's statement: "After the [first two] explosions there was no fire in the hall.... The glass was knocked out. The walls were damaged. There were many corpses along the walls. But the roof remained intact... The roof began to burn when they [the Russian forces] began to fire at it with some projectiles."[221]

"The most terrible thing occurred," Kesaev noted,

> when the ceiling began to burn. Here there are also questions... It [the roof] burned only from above, and then the roof fell down on those people, and they burned up precisely under it. In addition, there are the initial testimonies of the deputy of the State Duma, Vorob'eva, a doctor, concerning the charac-

---

[220]   Ivan Sukhov, "'My sdelaem vse vozmozhnoe, chtoby ustanovit' istinu,'" Vremya.ru, 28 June 2005. See also the discussion of the role of the Alfa and Vympel FSB *spetsnaz* units in, "Shturmovat' shkolu nachali tol'ko cherez 30 minut posle pervykh vzryvov," Vremya.ru, 6 September 2005.

[221]   Elena Milashina, "Kak shturmovali shkolu," *Novaya gazeta*, 7 October 2004.

ter of the burns encountered by the medics... In the history of the illness of each victim there are notes concerning burns from a substance similar to napalm.

So you believe that during the storm they used flamethrowers?

Yes, there were flamethrowers. The first batch of the flamethrowers that were used, which the member of the Federation Council Panteleev found in my presence, were given to the investigation. But the investigation simply washed them away.

You are saying that the investigation simply destroyed them?

No, it was done very simply. The wrong [serial] number [for the flamethrower] was written down, as if it were a mistake. Then when a *zapros* was submitted, it turned out there was no such batch... Later when they found other flamethrower parts, I advised the citizens to hand them over, but with that action being filmed by a television camera and with the numbers and everything written down according to protocol.[222]

The discovery of the flamethrowers served to incense the residents of Beslan.

In a meeting with the residents of Beslan [deputy Russian procurator general] Nikolai Shepel' declared that the flamethrowers had been used by the rebels [and not by the Russian forces]. The people did not believe him, since they understood perfectly that to fire from flamethrowers from within a building is impossible.... It was precisely then that the residents of Beslan conceived a strong distrust toward the Procuracy.[223]

Local residents testified that on the roofs of the buildings from which the flamethrowers had been fired "were located not rebels but employees of the [Russian] special services."[224] "People here," journalist Elena Milashina wrote from Beslan in December of 2004, "directly accuse our military of having used flamethrowers and having ignited the roof of the school thirty minutes after

---

[222] Vremya.ru, 28 June 2005.

[223] Ol'ga Bobrova, Elena Milashina, "Sensatsionnoe zayavlenie predstavitelya prokuratury," *Novaya gazeta*, 7 April 2005.

[224] *Ibid.*

the explosions in the gymnasium. This led to a fire, as a result of which the burning roof collapsed on the wounded but still living hostages."[225]

In an article appearing in the 7 October 2004 issue of *Novaya gazeta* leading military affairs analyst Pavel Felgengauer wrote that weapons which looked like *Shmel'* flamethrower/grenade launchers had been spotted on the roof of a building opposite the school. These weapons, he noted, had even been filmed by television crews.[226] Describing how a "Shmel'" works, "Chechnya Weekly" has observed:

> The *Shmel'* is a so-called 'thermo baric' weapon, similar to the controversial 'fuel-air' bombs used by the U.S. military in heavy combat. It disperses highly explosive droplets of petro-chemicals into a space occupied by the enemy—and then ig-nites them. The intense shock and heat of the resulting blast are devastating even to troops sheltering in entrenchments... One can only imagine the effect on a conventional building such as a school.[227]

In July 2005, the *Moscow Times* cited the opinion of Aleksandr Cherkasov, a senior member of the Memorial human rights organization, that Russia in its assault on the school apparently violated an international convention banning the use of incendiary weapons: "Although classified as a flamethrower," The *Times* wrote,

> the *Shmel'* in fact launches rocket-propelled projectiles... The *Shmel'* has three modifications: the RPO-A, whose shells ex-plode; the RPO-Z, whose shells are incendiary; and the RPO-D, whose shells create smoke. The commandos used the RPO-A type, [deputy procurator general] Shepel' told report-ers on July 12 [2005]. Its shells contain fuel-air explosives that on detonation form a ball of fire, creating a powerful blast ef-fect. Shepel' said the fire lasts only a split second, while expo-

---

[225]   Elena Milashina, "Logika 'Shmelei,'" *Novaya gazeta*, 20 December 2004.
[226]   Fel'gengauer, "'Shmel'" i svin'i."
[227]   *Chechnya Weekly*, 11 October 2004.

sure of three to five seconds is required to inflict burns on a person or set fire to a building.[228]

Shepel's comments evoked derision on the part of a number of Russian commentators. As Anatolii Ermolin, a State Duma deputy and a former commander of the *Vympel'* FSB special forces unit, declared: "To claim that the roof could not ignite from the use of a *Shmel'* is nonsense. Any explosion can cause a fire."[229]

The issue of the use of flamethrowers in the storming of the school came up in the conversation President Putin held with four Beslan Mothers on 2 September 2005. Putin, the Mothers subsequently recalled, read from a *spravka* (presumably prepared by the General Procuracy) that the flamethrower in question did not have an incendiary effect.

> We [the four Mothers] then said to the president: 'Let the flamethrower be called a water cannon. But we discovered flamethrowers at the crime scene. With two strips (RPO-A) and with three (RPO-Z), we have all the parts. That is, during the storming of the school both thermo baric and incendiary ones were used.' To this the president said: 'But they were firing from flamethrowers not at the gymnasium but at the school.' To which I [Susanna Dudieva] said: 'Vladimir Vladimirovich! In the school not one classroom was burned, not one window opening bears a trace from a flamethrower. Not one wall was burned through by a flamethrower. Only the gymnasium burned, which means that the flamethrower was fired only at the gymnasium. And there were no other shots [from a flamethrower]. I know how a flamethrower acts. I have read the literature on it and have read that it is used to destroy a sniper. Let's admit that.[230]

228 Anatoly Medetsky and Yana Voitova, "A reversal over Beslan only fuels speculation," *Moscow Times*, 21 July 2005.
229 "Zdanie polnost'yu razrusheno, no ne zagorelos'," Gazeta.ru, 12 July 2005.
230 "Vladimir Kolesnikov."

An expert on explosives who had examined the Beslan school after it had been stormed by Russian forces told journalist Svetlana Meteleva:

> Judging by the diameter of the openings in the wall, the explosions were rather localized. Not one of them could have produced the collapse of the roof, nor a broad-scale fire. And from examining the place of occurrence there emerges with all obviousness the conclusion: the hostages who were present in the gymnasium were literally buried under the collapsed roofing, after which they burned up.
> *And what could have been the reason for the fire?*
> The most likely one is the use of a flamethrower. If, say, someone outside the building decided that there was a rebel-sniper on the roof and fired at him from a flamethrower, the ensuing events look at least logical. The roofing would immediately have begun to burn and virtually any detonation would have been sufficient for its collapse—[say] a shot from an armored vehicle directed at the gymnasium... In the protocol of the examination of the place of occurrence, which was commenced at 7:00 a.m. on 4 September, it is clearly stated: the roofing of the gymnasium is missing. That is—I underline—the question concerns not only some burned out or fallen sections but the roof in its entirety. Such a result would not have been elicited by two or three explosions.[231]

According to Stanislav Kesaev, the explosion occurred in the region of the attic located above the gymnasium. It was in the attic that the terrorists had made a hole in the roof and set up an extremely elaborate sniper's nest, fortified "with bricked-in areas and surrounded inside with sacks of sand."[232] It seems likely therefore that the Russian special forces were attempting at about 1:30 p.m. on 3 September to take out a heavily defended enemy position located on the roof before launching a full-scale assault on the building. Like the use of a special gas at Nord-Ost in October of 2002, this action had unexpected and highly lethal consequences.

---

[231]   Meteleva, "Beslan bez grifov," part I, Mk.ru, 24 May 2005.

[232]   Elena Milashina, "Vyshe nekuda," *Novaya gazeta*, 5 September 2005.

In November 2005, while testifying at the Kulaev trial, Beslan police officer Chermen Khachirov "confirmed the version of the victims that at the moment of the storm soldiers were shooting at the school from flamethrowers. Khachirov was a witness of how, thirty minutes after the [first] explosion occurred in the gymnasium, they began, from an adjacent five-story building, to shoot at the school from flamethrowers. 'They carried more than twenty *Shmel's* up there. I saw them myself,' [Khachirov said]."[233]

Tanks Fire at the School

The Russian Procuracy has adamantly insisted that tanks and grenade launchers were used during the assault on the school building only after all of the hostages had either died or been evacuated. Yurii Savel'ev, however, a Duma deputy from the Russian nationalist *Rodina* faction and a member of the Torshin Commission, has stated: "According to the official version, the tanks opened fire on School No. 1 when all of the [living] hostages had been evacuated from the building and there were only terrorists in the basement, that is, at about 8:30 p.m. However Yurii Savel'ev declared that he possesses more than twenty testimonies in which eyewitnesses maintain that three tanks were used... at about 1:30 p.m."[234]

Similar findings abound. In its draft report, the Kesaev commission concluded:

> In the materials of the criminal case...there is exhaustive information concerning the fact that a tank platoon of the 58th army was given over in subordination to the Special Purpose Center of the FSB of the Russian Federation. The order to use

---

[233] "Shtab byl, no ego ne bylo," Gazeta.ru, 15 November 2005. Another local police officer, Alan Khodikov, testified at the trial that he was personally "a witness of how at a minimum ten shots were fired at the school from flamethrowers." See Mariya Bondarenko, "Po shkole strelyali iz vsekh stvolov," *Nezavisiamaya gazeta*, 17 November 2005.

[234] "Yurii Savel'ev: Bolee 20 svidetelei utverzhdayut, chto tanki v Beslane strelyali dnem," Rodina.ru, 8 September 2005.

the flamethrowers and tanks was given by the head of the
Special Purpose Center, General Tikhonov.... The commission possesses sufficient facts to show that the flamethrowers
and tanks were employed during the day of 3 September at a
time when a large number of hostages were present in the
school.[235]

For its part, the journalistic team of *Der Spiegel* has stipulated that at precisely 1:30 p.m. on 3 September: "Two tanks have moved up, plus armored
vehicles, and lethal grenade-launchers and flamethrowers have been brought
into position. Hardly rescue equipment, a lot of equipment for waging war. MI-
24 helicopter gun-ships circle above."[236] One Beslan resident and eyewitness
of events has recalled: "The tanks began to fire between 1:00 p.m. and 2:00
p.m. [on 3 September]. They were also firing from grenade launchers."[237]

Citing the afore-mentioned classified report of the experts' commission, journalist Svetlana Meteleva has written:

> An aide to the military procurator of the Vladikavkaz [North
> Ossetiya] garrison, Major of Justice Eminov, having examined
> the report of an [alleged] crime contained in the actions of the
> soldiers of the units and sub-units of the 58th army of the North
> Caucasus Military District of the Russian Federation and of
> the 59th Special Purpose Brigade of the North Caucasus Dis-
> trict of the Internal Troops of the MVD of the Russian Federa-
> tion, ruled: during the storm of the school building and the
> freeing of the hostages, these personnel made use of the
> flamethrowers RPO-A *Shmel'*, RPG-25 grenade launchers
> and also a T-72 tank. These forms of weaponry and armor
> were employed in the course of the storm during the firing at
> the building on 3 September 2004, which could result in the
> death of the hostages or in their receipt of bodily harm of vari-
> ous degrees."[238]

---

[235]   Milashina, "Den' nenznaniya."
[236]   Buse, Fichtner, Kaiser, Klussmann, Mayr and Neef, "Putins Ground Zero."
[237]   Pravdabeslana.ru, X, 38.
[238]   Meteleva, "Beslan bez grifov," part I, Mk.ru, 24 May 2005.

Similarly, journalist Elena Milashina has reported that, during the storm of the school building, military units "made use of RPO-A *Shmel'* flamethrowers, grenade launchers and a T-72 tank. The soldiers of unit v/ch 12356 alone, in addition to employing seven flamethrowers, made use, during the storm, according to official statistics, of 7,210 bullets and 10 grenades, while seven shots were fired from a tank."[239]

As the burning roof was threatening to collapse upon the injured and stunned hostages, a group of the terrorists, led by Vladimir Khodov, who was shouting in Ossetiyan, herded those hostages who were still alive and able to walk out of the gymnasium and into the cafeteria that was situated on the first floor. At this point, tanks and Russian soldiers with automatic weapons began firing at the cafeteria according to the eyewitness testimony of a number of hostages who were present there.

An article published in *Kommersant* reports:

> Rima Kusraeva related how the rebels [in the cafeteria] placed women and children in the window openings and gave them curtains to wave. Waving the curtains like white flags, they were to show that they [the Russian forces] should not fire at the windows. 'Then there came up an armored vehicle from which three soldiers jumped out and began to fire at the windows. I myself saw how a woman fell, after which there was a mountain of corpses on the window-sill.'[240]

An item appearing in *Novaya gazeta* relates: "Several women and children were forced [by the terrorists] to stand on the window-sills and wave white school blouses. And to shout: 'Don't shoot at us!' On the window-sill stood my sister Lora and my daughter Diana and they were shouting. But who would hear them? Lora pushed my Diana down to the floor. One woman fainted. The rest, including Lora, were shot." The woman hostage "confidently maintains that our people [the Russian forces] shot them. And the medics con-

---

239 Milashina, "Kak shturmovali shkolu."
240 Farniev, "Po nam terroristy voobshche ne strelayali."

firmed that they were shot in the chest and not the back."[241] Another woman hostage has recalled: "There was a real war going on there [in the cafeteria]. They were firing at us from tanks. How do I know? I know how tanks shoot because I am from South Ossetiya. I witnessed a war there."[242]

The crisis was compounded by the late arrival of local emergency personnel. In his report concerning the fire, the North Ossetiyan minister for emergency situations, Dzgoev, notes that at 1:05 p.m., at the time of the initial explosion in the school, he reported that there was a fire in the building. "I was given a command to await further orders and was told not to set about extinguishing the fire."[243] It was not until 3:20 p.m. that Dzgoev was able to send seven fire engines to the school. It then took some time for the fire engines to arrive.

In their conversation with President Putin on 2 September 2005, the four Beslan Mothers present

> spoke about the actions of the firemen. Why did the command to put out the fire [in the gymnasium] come to the firemen forty minutes late, and why then did it then take another forty minutes for the firemen to make their way to the school? During those eighty minutes everyone there burned up... People should also bear responsibility for this, for the fact that there was not an immediate extinguishing of the fire and for the fact that the units of the firemen were not prepared. The president said: 'Yes, unquestionably.'[244]

[241]   Milashina, "Kak shmturmovali shkolu."
[242]   Pravdabeslana.ru, XIII, 17.
[243]   Meteleva, "Beslan bez grifov," part III, Mk.ru, 26 May 2005.
[244]   "Vladimir Kolesnikov."

Aftermath

When all of the firing had ceased early in the morning of 4 September 2004, a reported 317 hostages lay dead, including 186 children. Most of them had been incinerated under the burning rubble of the collapsed roof of the gymnasium. Ten soldiers from the Russian *spetsnaz* had also been killed by the terrorists as had two representatives of the Ministry for Emergency Situations. Thirty-two terrorists likewise lay dead, while a still to be determined number of them, including, evidently, the Colonel, had succeeded in escaping. One or perhaps as many as four terrorists—including, according to some reports, Vladimir Khodov—had been captured.

At about 5:00 a.m. on 4 September,

> Putin arrived in Beslan. No-one met him at the airport except for his personal guard. From the airport the president immediately went to the district clinical hospital, where he was joined by the head of North Ossetiya, Aleksandr Dzasokhov. The two then visited all of the rooms containing victims... He went up to the badly wounded but still conscious principal of School No. 1, Lidiya Tsalieva. Having stayed in the hospital for thirty minutes, the president then attended a session of the operational headquarters to free the hostages, located in the town administration building.[245]

In attendance at this meeting were: the first deputy director of the FSB, Vladimir Pronichev; the minister for emergency situations, Sergei Shoigu; the deputy procurator general Sergei Fridinskii; the commander of the Fifty-eighth army General Sobolev; the head of the FSB for North Ossetiya, Valerii Andreev; and the minister of internal affairs of North Ossetiya, Kazbek Dzantiev.

Looking directly into the camera of state television's Channel 1, Putin then declared: "We examined all possible variants and did not ourselves plan an action using force. Events developed very quickly and unexpectedly, and the

---

[245] "Putin ne doekhal do razrushennoi shkoly," Gazeta.ru, 5 September 2004.

personnel of the special services manifested particular courage." He also voiced his opinion that the aim of the terrorists had been "to sow inter-ethnic enmity to blow up the entire North Caucasus."[246] Then, apparently without visiting the site of the ruined school, Putin returned to Moscow.

Later in the day, Putin addressed the nation on state television: "To speak is difficult and bitter," he began. "A terrible tragedy has taken place on our land.... We live in the conditions formed after the collapse of an enormous, great state [the USSR]... We exhibited weakness, and the weak are beaten." Putin concluded by announcing that, "in the very near future a complex of measures will be prepared toward strengthening the unity of the country."[247] The decision to abolish the election of Russian governors, it emerged, was one of the measures he had in mind.

On 13 September 2004, apparently responding to intense anger on the part of the surviving hostages and the relatives of those who had perished in the school, "Vladimir Putin removed from their posts the minister of internal affairs of North Ossetiya, Kazbek Dzantiev, and the head of the FSB of the republic, Valerii Andreev." In early 2005, however, it was reported that both of these generals had received prestigious new posts: "Dzantiev became the deputy commander of the internal troops of the Moscow Military District, while Andreev received the post of deputy head of the Academy of the FSB of the Russian Federation."[248] In mid-2005 it was announced that FSB first deputy director Vladimir Pronichev, the man who had de facto overseen the storming of the school, had been promoted to the rank of four-star general.[249]

In September 2005, journalist Mariya Mstislavskaya accurately summed up the gaping differences obtaining between the "official" interpretation of the Beslan events being articulated by the Russian General Procuracy and the

---

246   *Ibid.*

247   "Vladimir Putin vystupil v subbotu s obrashcheniem k natsii v svyazi s tragediei v Beslane," Newsru.com, 4 September 2004.

248   Panyushkin, "My khotim dokazat', chto vlasti vinovaty v gibeli detei."

249   "Shpionov zamenili narkokur'ery," *Argumenty i fakty*, 1 June 2005.

view being advanced by both the Kesaev commission and the Beslan Mothers. "In essence," she wrote,

> the version of the [official] investigation is a simple one: there were 32 terrorists in all, they brought all of their weapons with them, they advanced indistinct demands, and during the storm they were all killed—with the exception of Kulaev. Both the police and the FSB didn't do all that badly: although they failed to notice the terrorists and let them into Beslan, they didn't permit any of them to leave. The authorities showed themselves in good light: they created an operational headquarters, they entered into negotiations with the terrorists, and they did everything possible to avoid a storm. And the storm began when the terrorists began to shoot in the backs of the fleeing hostages. And, of course, losses could not have been avoided.

In contrast to this "official" narrative, there is the version being put forward by the Kesaev commission and the Beslan Mothers:

> The relatives of those who perished in Beslan and several former hostages place the responsibility for the death of the people directly on the authorities and on the special services. Those who spoke as witnesses at the trial of Kulaev declared that at least several of the terrorists had succeeded in getting away. Many of the victims also maintain that the weapons were brought into the school in advance. And the majority of the victims, in their words, perished under the rubble of the roof of the gymnasium, burning up after the soldiers began to fire at the school from flamethrowers.[250]

On 20 October 2005, Russian deputy procurator general Vladimir Kolesnikov held a press conference in Vladikavkaz at which he announced that the general procuracy's investigation of the Beslan incident had been completed. "In the words of Kolesnikov, the special [Procuracy] group confirmed the version of the investigation on all disputed points—concerning how many rebels there

---

[250] Mariya Mstislavskaya, "Chelovecheskoe, slishkom chelovecheskoe," Lenta.ru, 13 September 2005.

were, how they arrived in Beslan, how they acted, and for what reason the storm began."[251] No significant new information, Kolesnikov underlined, had been turned up relating to the investigation.

Representatives of the Beslan Mothers, some of whose members had been denied entrance to the press conference, declared themselves completely dissatisfied with Kolesnikov's conclusions. Susanna Dudieva, a leader of the Mothers, stated:

> We do not agree with the investigation that the Kolesnikov group has conducted. We have once again become convinced that the Procuracy does not want to work with the facts, and that it seeks to justify its non-objective investigation on all the key points about which we have had questions, and to which we have not received answers. We will continue to insist that we are in disagreement with the investigation, and we will insist on another meeting with the president. We fail to understand why the Kolesnikov group came here at all.[252]

[251] "Genprokuratura soglasilas' sama s soboi," Vremya.ru, 21 October 2005.

[252] *Ibid.*

Bibliographical Update (December 2005)

On 29 November 2005, Stanislav Kesaev, chair of the North Ossetiyan parliamentary commission on Beslan, presented that body's findings at a session
of the regional parliament held in Vladikavkaz. The assembled deputies were
not given the written version of the commission's report. In delivering his oral
summary, Kesaev apologized to the deputies for the fact that copies of the
written report were not available, citing "certain mysterious technical problems."[253]

A leaked copy of the North Ossetiyan parliamentary commission's written report on Beslan revealed that it was considerably more critical of the federal
authorities than was Kesaev's oral summary of its findings. "The leaked [writ-
ten] report," the *Moscow Times* wrote,

> described federal authorities' response to the September 1-3,
> 2004 attack and hostage crisis as 'inept' and called on them to
> stop portraying conflict in the North Caucasus as part of the
> global terrorist threat. It also hinted strongly that the Septem-
> ber 3 storming of the school by federal forces was set off by
> shelling of the building from outside, a conclusion that contra-
> dicts prosecutors' explanation that a bomb planted by the at-
> tackers detonated accidentally. Copies of the report were not
> available at the North Ossetiyan legislature on [29 November]
> when inquiry chairman Stanislav Kesaev...presented a sum-
> mary of its findings to lawmakers, victims' relatives and re-
> porters.[254]

A leaked copy of the full written version of the Kesaev Commission's report
was posted at the website of the newspaper *Novaya gazeta* on 29 November
2005. It may be found at this URL: http://www.novayagazeta.ru/rassled2/
beslan/article/article2.shtml

---

[253]   Valery Dzutsev, "Beslan Inquiry Criticizes Agencies," *Moscow Times*, 30 November
2005.
[254]   Nabi Abdullaev, "Leaked Beslan Report More Critical," *Moscow Times*, 1 December
2005.

On 30 November, the organization "Voice of Beslan," which includes in its membership a number of the mothers of children who perished in the terrorist incident, issued an appeal to the President of the United States; the Congress of the United States; the heads of the member states of the European Union; the European Parliament; the editors of all world television companies, information agencies, newspapers and journals that have shed light on the Beslan events; and all Russian journalists who had worked in Beslan during the period 1-3 September 2005. The addressees were asked to exert all of their power and influence to ensure that an objective investigation of the Beslan tragedy is conducted.[255]

Highlighting the political significance of the Beslan Mothers, the distinguished sociologist and polling specialist Yurii Levada noted that for the time being Russian citizens are generally not prepared to engage in protest activities. Only the Beslan Mothers, he remarked, have been able to become a truly influential protest organization in Russia. But, he added, "the attitude [of the authorities] toward them is both frightened and spiteful. They seek to scare them [the Mothers] and to split their ranks."[256]

---

[255] "Obrashchenie obshchestvennoi organizatsii 'Golos Beslana,'" Ej.ru, 30 November 2005.

[256] Cited in Aleksandr Kolesnichenko, "Stabil'no nedovol'nye," Newizv.ru, 2 December 2005.

II   The October 2002 Moscow Hostage-Taking Incident

On 6 November 2002, a meeting was held in Moscow of the Public Committee to Investigate the Circumstances Behind the Explosions of the Apartment
Buildings in Moscow and the Ryazan Exercises (all of which occurred in September 1999). The meeting took place at the Andrei Sakharov Center, and
among those present were the committee's chairman, Duma Deputy Sergei
Kovalev, its deputy chairman, Duma Deputy Sergei Yushenkov (assassinated
on 17 April 2003), lawyer Boris Zolotukhin, writer Aleksandr Tkachenko, journalist Otto Latsis, and human rights activist Valerii Borshchev. After the meeting had concluded, the members of the committee took a formal decision to
"broaden its mandate" and to include the Moscow hostage-taking episode of
23-26 October 2002—and especially the actions of the Russian special services during that period—as an additional subject of inquiry coming under the
committee's purview.[1]

An Unusual Kind of "Joint Venture"?

The following is an attempt to make some sense out of the small torrent of information that exists concerning the October 2002 events at Dubrovka. In my
opinion, the original plan for the terrorist action at and around Dubrovka bears
a strong similarity to the campaign of terror bombings unleashed upon Moscow and other Russian urban centers (Buinaksk, Volgodonsk) in September
of 1999. In both cases there is strong evidence of official involvement in, and
manipulation of, key actions; so the question naturally arises as to whether

---

[1]   Grani.ru, 6 November 2002. The author would like to thank Robert Otto for his
exceptionally generous bibliographical assistance and for his most useful comments
on a draft of this essay. Peter Reddaway also made a number of remarkably inci-
sive comments on the manuscript. Lawrence Uzzell, too, provided constructive and
helpful criticism. The author is, of course, solely responsible for the final version of
this essay.

Vladimir Putin in any way sanctioned them. Although there is additional evidence bearing on Putin's possible role, this paper will take an agnostic position on the issue, and will also not review it.

The October 2002 hostage-taking episode in a large theater containing close to 1,000 people was evidently, at least in its original conception, to have been preceded and accompanied by terror bombings claiming the lives of perhaps hundreds of Muscovites, a development that would have terrorized and enraged the populace of the entire country. However, in view of the suspicious connections and motivations of the perpetrators of this incident, as well as the contradictory nature of the actions of the authorities, it would seem appropriate to envisage this operation as representing a kind of "joint venture" (on, for example, the model of the August 1999 incursion into Dagestan) involving elements of the Russian special services and also radical Chechen leaders such as Shamil Basaev and Movladi Udugov.

Only a few individuals among the special services and the Chechen extremist leadership would likely have known of the existence of this implicit deal. Both "partners" had a strong motive to derail the movement occurring in Russia, and being backed by the West, to bring about a negotiated settlement to the Chechen conflict. Both also wanted to blacken the reputation of the leader of the Chechen separatist moderates, Aslan Maskhadov. In addition, the Chechen extremists clearly saw their action as a kind of ambitious fund-raiser aimed at attracting financial support from wealthy donors in the Gulf states and throughout the Muslim world (hence the signs displayed in Arabic, the non-traditional [for Chechens] garb of the female terrorists, and so on). The Russian authorities, for their part, had a propitious chance to depict the conflict in Chechnya as a war against an Al-Qaeda-type Chechen terrorism, a message that could be expected to play well abroad, and especially in the United States.

As in the case of the 1999 terror bombings, meticulous planning—including the use of "cut-outs," false documents, and the secret transport of weapons and explosives to Moscow from the North Caucasus region—underlay the preparation for this terrorist assault. In this instance, however, the perpetrators were to be seen as Chechens of a "Wahhabi" orientation whose modus operandi was to recall that of the notorious Al-Qaeda and the Taliban.

Once the operation had moved into its active stage, however, strange and still not fully explained developments began to occur. An explosion at a McDonald's restaurant in southwest Moscow on 19 October immediately riveted the attention of the Moscow Criminal Investigation (MUR)—an elite unit of the regular police—which then moved swiftly to halt the activity of the terrorists. The explosion at the McDonald's restaurant was, fortunately, a small one, and caused the death of only a single person. Two large bombs set to explode before the assault on Dubrovka was launched failed to detonate. Likewise a planned bombing incident at a large restaurant in Pushkin Square in the center of the capital failed to take place.

In my opinion, the most likely explanation for these "technical" failures lies in acts of intentional sabotage committed by some of the terrorists. What remains unclear at this juncture is why certain individuals among the terrorists chose to render the explosive devices incapable of functioning. One key point, however, seems clear: The Chechen extremist leaders felt no pressing need to blow up or shoot hundreds of Russian citizens. They were aware that such actions might so enrage the Russian populace that it would then have supported any military actions whatever, including a possible full-scale extermination of the Chechen people. So what Shamil Basaev, Aslambek Khaskhanov, and their comrades in arms seem to have done is, in a sense, to outplay the special services in a game of chess. Most of the bombs, it turns out, were actually fakes, while the few women's terrorist belts that did actually contain explosives were of danger primarily to the women themselves. As Russian security affairs correspondent Pavel Felgengauer has rightly suggested, the aim of the extremist leaders seems to have been to force the Russian special services to kill ethnic Russians on a large scale, and that is what happened.[2] Only an adroit cover-up by the Russian authorities pre-

---

[2]   Sovsekretno.ru, November 2002.

vented the full extent (conceivably more than 200 deaths) of the debacle from becoming known.

A central question to be resolved by future researchers is whether or not the Russian special forces planning an assault on the theater building at Dubrovka were aware that virtually all of the bombs located there—including all of the powerful and deadly bombs—were in fact incapable of detonating. If the special forces were aware of this, then there was clearly no need to employ a potentially lethal gas, which, it turned out, caused the deaths of a large number of the hostages. The special forces could have relatively easily and rapidly overwhelmed the lightly armed terrorists. Moreover, if they were in fact aware that the bombs were "dummies," then the special forces obviously had no need to kill all of the terrorists, especially those who were asleep from the effects of the gas. It would, one would think, have made more sense to take some of them alive.

Pressure Builds For a Negotiated Settlement with the Chechen Separatists

In the months preceding the terrorist act at the Dubrovka theater, which was putting on a popular musical, "Nord-Ost," the Kremlin leadership found itself coming under heavy political pressure both within Russia and in the West to enter into high-level negotiations with the moderate wing of the Chechen separatists headed by Aslan Maskhadov, who was elected Chechen president in 1997. Public-opinion polls in Russia showed that a continuation of the Chechen conflict was beginning to erode Putin's generally high approval ratings. With parliamentary elections scheduled for just over a year's time (in December 2003), this represented a worrisome problem for the Kremlin. In a poll taken by the All-Russia Center for the Study of Public Opinion (VTsIOM), whose findings were reported on 8 October, respondents were asked "how the situation in Chechnya has changed since V. Putin was elected president."[3] Thirty percent of respondents believed that the situation had "gotten better," but 43 percent opined that it had "not changed," while 21 percent thought that it had "gotten worse." These results were significantly lower than Putin's ratings in other categories. In similar fashion, a September 2002 Russia-wide poll taken by VTsIOM found 56 percent of respondents favoring peace negotiations as a way to end the Chechen conflict while only 34 percent supported the continuing of military actions.[4]

On 16-19 August 2002, key discussions had occurred in the Duchy of Liechtenstein involving two former speakers of the Russian parliament, Ivan Rybkin and Ruslan Khasbulatov, as well as two deputies of the Russian State Duma: journalist and leading "democrat" Yurii Shchekochikhin (died, possibly from the effects of poison, on 3 July 2003) and Aslambek Aslakhanov, a retired Interior Ministry general who had been elected to represent Chechnya in the Duma. Representing separatist leader Maskhadov at the talks was Chechen Deputy Prime Minister Akhmed Zakaev. The talks in Liechtenstein had been organized by the American Committee for Peace in Chechnya (executive director, Glen Howard), one of whose leading figures was former U.S. national security adviser Zbigniew Brzezinski. The meetings in Liechtenstein were intended to restore the momentum that had been created by earlier talks held at Sheremetevo-2 Airport outside of Moscow between Zakaev and Putin's plenipotentiary presidential representative in the Southern Federal District, retired military General Viktor Kazantsev, on 18 November 2001.[5] Efforts to resuscitate the talks had failed to achieve any success because of the strong opposition of the Russian side.

Following the stillborn initiative of November 2001, the Kremlin had apparently jettisoned the idea of holding any negotiations whatsoever with moder-

---

3   Posted on Polit.ru, 8 October 2002, by VTsIOM polling specialist L. A. Sedov.

4   Yurii Levada, "Reiting voiny," *Novoe vremya*, 5 November 2002.

5   See Yevgeniya Borisova, "Kazantsev's Ball Now in Rebels' Court," *The Moscow Times*, 20 November 2001. For an informative account by Shchekochikhin of a long conversation he had with Zakaev in Liechtenstein, see Yurii Shchekochikhin, *Zabytaya Chechnya* (Moscow: Olimp, 2003), 248-259. Zakaev describes, inter alia, details of the peace agreement he had largely come to with retired general Kazantsev.

ate separatists in favor of empowering its handpicked candidate for Chechen leader, former mufti Akhmad Kadyrov. This tactic, said to be backed by Aleksandr Voloshin, the then presidential chief of staff, soon became known as "Chechenization." Other elements among the top leadership of the presidential administration, such as two deputy chiefs of staff, Viktor Ivanov—a former deputy director of the FSB—and Igor Sechin, as well as certain leaders in the so-called power ministries, for example, Federal Security Service (FSB) Director Nikolai Patrushev, were reported to be adamantly opposed both to Chechenization and, even more so, to holding talks with moderate separatists; what they wanted was aggressively to pursue the war to a victorious conclusion.[6] If that effort took years more to achieve, then so be it.

In a path-breaking report on the meetings in Liechtenstein, a leading journalist who frequently publishes in the weekly *Moskovskie novosti*, Sanobar Shermatova, wrote that the participants had discussed two peace plans: the so-called "Khasbulatov plan" and the so-called "Brzezinski plan."[7] Eventually, she went on, the participants decided to merge the two plans into a "Liechtenstein plan," which included elements of both. Khasbulatov's plan was based on the idea of granting to Chechnya "special status," with international guarantees being provided by the Organization for Security and Cooperation in Europe (OSCE) and by the Council of Europe. Under Khasbulatov's plan, Chechnya would be free to conduct its own internal and foreign policies, with the exception of those functions that it voluntarily delegated to the Russian Federation. The republic was to remain within Russian borders and was to preserve Russian citizenship and currency.

Under the "Brzezinski plan," Chechens would "acknowledge their respect for the territorial integrity of the Russian Federation," while Russia, for its part,

---

[6]   On this group, see "Chekisty vo vlasti," *Novaya gazeta*, 14 July 2003.

[7]   Sanobar Shermatova, "Chechen Plan Hammered Out," *Institute for War and Peace Reporting*, 30 August 2002. The "Khasbulatov plan" appeared as a prefix entitled "Plan mira dlya Chechenskoi respubliki" in Ruslan Khasbulatov, *Vzorvannaya zhizn'* (Moscow: Graal, 2002). The so-called "Brzezinski plan" appeared as: Zbigniew Brzezinski, Alexander Haig, and Max Kampelman, "The Way to Chechen Peace," *The Washington Post*, 21 June 2002.

would "acknowledge the right of the Chechens to political, though not national, self-determination." A referendum would be held under which "Chechens would be given the opportunity to approve the constitutional basis for extensive self-government" modeled on what the Republic of Tatarstan currently enjoys. Russian troops would remain stationed on Chechnya's southern borders. "International support," the plan stressed, "must be committed to a substantial program of economic reconstruction, with a direct international presence on the ground in order to promote the rebuilding and stabilization of Chechen society." The authors of this plan underlined that "Maskhadov's endorsement of such an approach would be essential because of the extensive support he enjoys within Chechen society."

On 17 October 2002—just six days before the terrorist incident at Dubrovka— the website Grani.ru, citing information that had previously appeared in the newspaper *Kommersant*, reported that new meetings of the Liechtenstein group were scheduled to be held in two weeks' time.[8] Duma Deputy Aslakhanov and separatist Deputy Premier Zakaev were planning to meet one-on-one in Switzerland in order "seriously to discuss the conditions which could lead to negotiations." Former speakers Rybkin and Khasbulatov, the website added, would also be taking part in the negotiations. In mid-October, Aslakhanov emphasized in a public statement: "President Putin has not once expressed himself against negotiations with Maskhadov. To the contrary, in a conversation with me, he expressed doubt whether there was a real force behind Maskhadov. Would the people follow after him?" This question put by Putin to Aslakhanov, *Kommersant-vlast'* reporter Olga Allenova observed, "was perceived in the ranks of the separatists as a veiled agreement [by Putin] to negotiations."[9]

On 10 September 2002, former Russian Prime Minister Yevgenii Primakov had published an essay entitled "Six Points on Chechnya" on the pages of the official Russian government newspaper *Rossiiskaya gazeta* in which he

---

[8]   Grani.ru, 17 October 2002.
[9]   Olga Allenova, "Terrorizm i zakhvat posle antrakta," *Kommersant vlast*, 28 October 2002.

stressed the urgent need to conduct "negotiations with [separatist] field commanders or at least some of them."[10] "This struggle," Primakov insisted, "can
be stopped only through negotiations. Consequently elections in Chechnya
cannot be seen as an alternative to negotiations." Primakov also underlined
his conviction that "the [Russian] military must not play the dominant role in
the settlement." In an interview which appeared in the 4 October 2002 issue
of *Nezavisimaya gazeta*, Salambek Maigov, co-chairman of the Antiwar
Committee of Chechnya, warmly praised Primakov's "Six Points," noting,
"Putin and Maskhadov can find compromise decisions. But the problem is
that there are groups in the Kremlin which hinder this process."

During September 2002, Grani.ru reported that both Maigov and former
Duma Speaker Ivan Rybkin were supporting a recent suggestion by Primakov
that "the status of Finland in the [tsarist] Russian Empire can suit the Chechen Republic."[11] Another possibility, Rybkin pointed out, would be for
Chechnya to be accorded "the status of a disputed territory, such as was held
by the Aland Islands [of Finland], to which both Sweden and Finland had earlier made claims." A broad spectrum of Russian political leaders—from "de-
mocrats" like Grigorii Yavlinskii, Boris Nemtsov, and Sergei Kovalev to Gennadii Zyuganov, leader of the Communist Party of the Russian Federation—
had, Rybkin said, expressed an interest in such models.

During the course of a lengthy interview—whose English translation appeared
on the separatist website chechenpress.com on 23 October (the day of the
seizure of the hostages in Moscow)—President Maskhadov warmly wel-
comed the intensive efforts being made to bring about a negotiated settlement to the Chechen conflict: "In Dr. Brzezinski's plan," Maskhadov commented,

> we see the concern of influential forces in the United States....
> We have a positive experience of collaboration with Ivan Pet-

---

[10]   Yevgenii Primakov, "Shest' punktov po Chechne," *Rossiiskaya gazeta*, 10 September 2002.

[11]   Grani.ru 17 September 2002.

rovich Rybkin [the reference is to the year 1997, when Rybkin was secretary of the Russian Security Council].... If Yevgenii Primakov speaks of the possibility of a peace resolution, it is a good sign.... The Chechen party would willingly collaborate with the academician [Primakov]. And, finally, with respect to Ruslan Khasbulatov's plan,... we welcome the actions of Khasbulatov.... This plan can be the subject for negotiations.

It appears that Maskhadov was at this time also engaging in secret talks with a high-ranking representative of President Putin. "Into contact with the president of [the Chechen Republic of] Ichkeria, who was on the wanted list," journalist Sanobar Shermatova reported in February of 2003, "there entered such a high-ranking [Russian] official that he was threatened by no unpleasantness whatsoever by the law-enforcement organs for communicating with the Chechen leader."[12]

The FSB Suppresses a Promising Peacemaking Effort

It emerged at this time that Putin had also permitted his special representative for human rights in Chechnya, Abdul-Khakim Sultygov, an ethnic Chechen, to meet with Chechen deputies who had been elected to the separatist parliament in 1997. On 13 October, 10 days before the hostage-taking incident at Dubrovka, Sultygov met in Znamenskoe, the district center of Nadterechnyi District in northern Chechnya, with 14 such deputies. Observers from the OSCE's mission in Znamenskoe were said to have been involved in preparing the meeting. At the meeting, Sultygov and the Chechen deputies discussed ways of bringing about a political regulation of the crisis and also the need to observe human rights in Chechnya.

---

[12] Sanobar Shermatova, "Mirotvortsy pod kovrom," *Moskovskie novosti*, No. 6, 18 February 2003. Subsequently Shermatova reported that the high-level talks had been conducted "in one of the republics of the North Caucasus." ("Shestero iz baraevskikh," *Moskovskie novosti*, 29 April 2003). Writing in "Po-amerikanski ne poluchaetsya?" in the 5 August 2003 issue of *Moskovskie novosti*, Shermatova added: "At the very time when Moscow was accusing Maskhadov of having organized the terrorist act at Dubrovka, he, according to our information, was located in a secure place in one of the republics of the North Caucasus."

According to a website associated with the leading Russian human rights organization Memorial (http://www.hro.org), the FSB of Chechnya headed by
General Sergei Babkin (an organization in strict subordination to the FSB of
Russia) moved aggressively to quash this nascent peacemaking effort.[13] A
mere 100 meters away from Sultygov's office in Znamenskoe, hro.org reported, the separatist parliamentarians were taken into custody by armed
masked men, who then escorted them to the central FSB office in Nad-
terechnoe. Each separatist deputy was then interrogated by the FSB department head, Mairbek Khusuev, who subjected them, inter alia, to "insulting
remarks." Sultygov, Memorial concluded, came to understand "the decisive-
ness of his [FSB] opponents who were not deterred by the presence of international observers [from the OSCE]. The breaking off of negotiations...is evidently profitable for the adherents of the force variant."

As this incident demonstrates, key elements among the *siloviki*, or power ministries, were adamantly opposed to conducting peace negotiations with separatists and, moreover, to bringing an end to a war that was serving as a
source of promotions in rank and of lucrative "financial flows." It seems likely
that President Putin's intention was to project the appearance of a willingness
to acquiesce to the peacemaking activities of Aslakhanov, Sultygov and others, as a largely symbolic sop to the Europeans. On 21 October, two days before the Dubrovka incident, the president's official spokesman, Sergei
Yastrzhembskii, announced that there could be no negotiations on the conditions set by the rebels and that "only the official representative of Russia, Viktor Kazantsev, is to conduct negotiations with the separatists, while the remaining initiatives [such as those of Aslakhanov and Sultygov] are deemed to
be personal ones."[14]

The involvement of the OSCE in the events in Znamenskoe was an indication
that some Western European governments (as well as the United States)
were becoming involved in the quest for a solution to a seemingly intractable

---

13   Hro.org, 19 October 2002.
14   Allenova, "Terrorizm i zakhvat posle antrakta."

conflict. At the time of the Dubrovka episode, Denmark was serving as host for a two-day conference on Chechnya attended by some 100 separatists, human rights activists, and parliamentarians. Maskhadov's spokesman, Zakaev, was one of the event's featured speakers.[15]

At this time, other pressures, too, were being brought to bear on the Kremlin to enter into peace negotiations. To cite one example, on 18 October, five days before the Dubrovka incident, a conference entitled "Chechen Dead End: Where to Seek the Peace?" was held at the centrally located Hotel *Rossiya* in Moscow.[16] The conference had been organized by the Committee of Soldiers' Mothers of Russia. Among those who addressed the congress were Duma faction leader Nemtsov, former Duma Speaker Rybkin, Maigov, and Akhmed-Khadzhi Shamaev, the (pro-Moscow) mufti of the Chechen Republic.

It should be underscored that there also existed a significant group of Chechens who complemented the influential and retrograde elements of the FSB and other power structures on the Russian side adamantly opposed to a peace settlement with Maskhadov. These elements consisted of extremist or "Wahhabi" elements among the separatists. The central figure of this group within Chechnya was, of course, the legendary field commander Shamil Basaev, and, abroad, said to be living in the Gulf states, Basaev's partners, the former Chechen First Deputy Premier and Minister of Information Movladi Udugov and former acting President Zelimkhan Yandarbiev. On 4 October, a website affiliated with this group, Kavkaz Center (http://www.kavkaz.org), lambasted the involvement of Ruslan Khasbulatov and Aslambek Aslakhanov in the peace process. Khasbulatov, the website remarked scathingly, "wants to be the Kremlin's only 'man' in Chechnya and to have a full mandate for talks with rebel president Aslan Maskhadov," while Aslakhanov, in the website's view, was serving as Khasbulatov's "power-wielding" assistant seeking to gain control of all the Russian forces in Chechnya.[17]

---

15 *The Moscow Times*, 31 October 2002.
16 Grani.ru, 18 October.
17 Kavkaz-Tsentr, translated by *BBC Monitoring*, 4 October 2002.

Setting the Stage

One of the key questions confronting any examination of the Dubrovka events remains how it was possible that such a collection of suspicious individuals could gather and furtive activities occur in and around Moscow over a period of months. Moreover, the provenance of some of the players—coupled with reports that several of the participants among the hostage takers had already been in the custody of the Russian authorities—only serves to sharpen this issue.

The Terrorist Action Takes Shape

The activities that culminated in the hostage seizure took place over a period of more than half a year. In February of 2002, eight months before the hostage-taking incident, two Chechen terrorists, "Zaurbek" (real name: Aslambek Khaskhanov) and "Abubakar," also known as "Yasir" (real name: Ruslan Elmurzaev), set the future terrorist act at Dubrovka in motion when they approached a third Chechen, Akhyad Mezhiev, in Ingushetiya, where Mezhiev was wont to make regular visits to a cousin living in that republic.[18] Mezhiev had been born in the village of Makhkety, in the Vedeno District of Chechnya, but had managed to acquire legal residency in Moscow even before the first Chechen war. "In terms of an ultimatum, they demanded that Mezhiev assist them, threatening otherwise to take revenge against his relatives living in Chechnya." Mezhiev was provided with a false internal passport, and his brother, Alikhan, was also drawn into the plot. Later Khaskhanov was to provide Alikhan with $2,500 with which to buy two vehicles intended to be used as car bombs. (These vehicles were said to have been purchased during the period August-September 2002.)

According to a June 2003 statement made by the then chief procurator of the

---

[18]   Aleksandr Khinshtein, "Glavnyi terrorist 'Nord-Osta'," *Moskovskii komsomolets*, 23 May 2003; and Zinaida Lobanova, "Tolko on otvetit za 'Nord-Ost'?" *Komsomol'skaya pravda*, 22 April 2003.

city of Moscow, Mikhail Avdyukov, Aslambek Khaskhanov had been closely acquainted with terrorist leader Shamil Basaev. "Still in 2001, in the village of Starye Atagi," Avdyukov related, "he [Khaskhanov] received an assignment from Basaev, through a certain Edaev, to commit a series of terrorist acts in Moscow. Later when Edaev had been killed... Shamil Basaev himself directly confirmed the assignment to Khaskhanov. The terrorist acts were to consist of a series of 'actions of intimidation.'"[19] Avdyukov's statement continued: "He [Khaskhanov] was commanded to head a group and carry out in Moscow four large terrorist acts with the use of explosives in crowded places. In addition to himself, the group also consisted of Aslan Murdalov, the brothers Alikhan and Akhyad Mezhiev, Khampasha Sobraliev, and Arman Menkeev. All of them are now under arrest."

In April 2002, another member of the Chechen terrorist group, the already-mentioned Khampash Sobraliev, purchased a substantial property at House No. 100 on Nosovikhinskii Highway in the village of Chernoe, Balashikhinskii District, Moscow Oblast. The asking price for the property was said to have been $20,000. A family of Chechens then moved in: "Pavel [i.e., Kham-pash]...and two young women." The two women appear to have been So-braliev's wife and sister. The family then erected a high fence around the property and began to receive visitors driving expensive foreign cars and large jeeps. Sobraliev's home soon became a hub of activity with the arrival of a former military-intelligence (GRU) operative. Arman Menkeev, a retired (December 1999) major in the GRU and a specialist, inter alia, in the making of explosives, moved in as a guest in the summerhouse on the property. (Khampash and the women were living in the main house.) The neighbors knew Menkeev as "Roma" and Sobraliev as "Pasha."[20]

---

[19]   "V Moskve gotovilos' chetyre 'Nord-Osta'," *Rossiiskaya gazeta*, 20 June 2003. Avdyukov was removed from his post in July 2003: "Prokuror Moskvy podal v ot-stavku," Grani.ru, 31 July 2003.

[20]   See Khinshtein, "Glavnyi terrorist 'Nord-Osta';" Andrei Skrobot, "Vzryvy v Moskve gotovyat v Podmoskovye," *Nezavisimaya gazeta*, 6 June 2003; and Zinaida Lo-banova and Andrei Red'kin, "Ne vinovny my! Baraev sam prishel," *Komsomol'skaya pravda*, 23 June 2003.

Menkeev's background and questions concerning his ultimate loyalties serve to highlight many of the problems connected with analyzing the Dubrovka events. According to an article posted in June of 2003 on the website Agentura.ru, Arman Menkeev is "a Russian officer, a major, and a former deputy commander of a [GRU] special-forces detachment." Menkeev, who had been born in 1963 to a Kazakh father and Chechen mother, had previously served as a member of "the famous Chuchkovskaya Brigade of the GRU special forces." During the 18 years in which he was in the GRU, Menkeev had served abroad and was said to speak Farsi. He had also fought with the Russian military during the first Chechen war (1994-96), during which he had received a military decoration for valor, had been wounded, and had "received the classification of an invalid." Menkeev is also reported by Agentura.ru to have prepared the "women martyrs' belts," the homemade grenades, and other explosive devices used by the Dubrovka hostage takers in October of 2002.[21] The weapons and explosives employed during October had been "transported to this house [in the village of Chernoe] straight from Chechnya in trucks containing boxes of apples."[22] (Other sources assert that they had been transported by vehicle from Ingushetiya, not Chechnya.)

The article in Agentura.ru directly raised the question of whether Menkeev was a traitor to Russia who was heeding the "voice of the blood" (of his Chechen mother) or whether he represented, instead, a loyal servant of Russia. The author noted that after Menkeev had been arrested in Chernoe by Russian police on 22 November 2002, FSB officers interrogating him at the Lefortovo Prison in Moscow had come to a decision to classify him as "loyal to the

---

21   Aleksandr Zheglov, "Pravitelstvu veren," Agentura.ru, 30 June 2003. This article is said by Agentura.ru to have first appeared in the newspaper *Den'*, 3 December 2003.

22   Zinaida Lobanova et al., "Naiden ment, pustivshii terroristov v 'Nord-Ost'," *Komsomol'skaya pravda*, 9 June 2003. An earlier report by Lobanova that appeared in the 22 April 2003 issue of the same newspaper had stated that the weapons and explosives had been transported to the capital from Ingushetiya in a truck loaded with watermelons and had then been kept in two rented garages in Moscow, one on *Leninskii prospekt* and one on *Ogorodnyi proezd*. It appears that the explosives were originally housed at the base in the village of Chernoe.

[Russian] government," adding mysteriously, "He knows how to keep a military and state secret."

By the summer of 2002, the terrorist conspiracy had begun to move into high gear. "For a certain time, the rebels tested [Akhyad] Mezhiev. Then, in the summer of 2002, they introduced him to his contact, Aslambek [Khaskhanov], and to the demolition specialist, Yasir,... who arrived specially in Ingushetiya from Chechnya to become acquainted with him. Yasir was introduced to the neophyte under the pseudonym of Abubakar." (Both names, we now know, were pseudonyms used by Ruslan Elmurzaev, who was at that time a resident of Moscow and not of Chechnya.) In August 2002, both Khaskhanov and Elmurzaev paid a visit to Mezhiev in Moscow. Responding to ads that he had read in a newspaper, "Mezhiev then purchased two unremarkable vehicles and passed the keys to them—as well as cell phones he had been instructed to purchase—to Aslambek, who arrived specially from Nazran [Ingushetiya]" to receive them.[23]

The activities of these Chechen terrorists in Moscow had not, it turned out, passed unnoticed. In fact, according to attorney Mikhail Trepashkin, not only were certain of these activities observed but the authorities were informed about them. However, the authorities then chose to take no action. Trepashkin, a former lieutenant colonel in the FSB turned dissident lawyer, was a controversial individual in his own right. In 1998, he had sued then FSB Director Nikolai Kovalev over his dismissal from the service and had participated in a November 1998 press conference together with another former FSB officer, Aleksandr Litvinenko, devoted to the subject of criminal activities occurring within the FSB. In 1999, Trepashkin had begun assisting the Sergei Kovalev commission in its investigation of the 1999 Moscow and Volgodonsk terror bombings.

According to Trepashkin's testimony, Elmurzaev ("Abubakar") and his associates operated in a gray zone where criminal activity routinely intersected with elements of Russian officialdom. In his "Statement" (*Spravka*), dated 23

---

23   Lobanova, "Tolko on otvetit za 'Nord-Ost'?"

March 2003, Trepashkin recalled: "Beginning in May of 2002, from people in the 'criminal world' there came information about a concentration of Chechens in the city of Moscow...such as had not been observed over the past two years."[24] From a retired secret-police officer who was working as a lawyer for several Chechen firms, Trepashkin learned that "Abdul" (a former field commander of Chechen terrorist leader Salman Raduev and of late separatist President Djokhar Dudaev) had appeared in the capital. "I also," Trepashkin continued,

> received information on 'Abubakar,' who, for an extensive period of time, had been living in the city of Moscow and had been earning a profit from firms based at the Hotel Salyut in the southwest of Moscow that no one was laying a hand on. Information had come even earlier that the Hotel Salyut was sending part of the funds to support the Chechen rebels. However, no one was carrying out any checking, since the shadowy funds were also being disseminated to several leaders of the [Russian] power structures. The Hotel Salyut was headed by two Chechens,... but their deputy was [retired] Lieutenant General of the USSR KGB Bogantsev. For this reason, no one [among the authorities] was laying a hand on 'Abubakar' in the hotel.

Following the Dubrovka incident, Trepashkin voluntarily turned over the information he had collected concerning "Abubakar" to the FSB, but the FSB reacted to this gesture by "trying to fabricate a criminal case against me."

In a later statement, dated 20 July 2003, Trespashkin added: "At the end of July-August 2002,... I received information about a concentration in the city of Moscow of armed Chechen extremists.... They were especially concentrated in the Southwest and Central districts of the city of Moscow." Trepashkin recalled that he had earlier taken "Abdul" into custody in Chechnya in 1995 but that a senior secret police official, Nikolai Patrushev [now head of the FSB],

---

24   For the text of Trepashkin's "Spravka," see "Tainstvennyi 'Abubakar'," Chechen-press.com, 31 July 2003.

and the then director of the FSK, Mikhail Barsukov, had "ordered me to leave him in peace.[25]

In a conversation with a retired FSB colonel, V.V. Shebalin, Trepashkin "pointed out to him that in Moscow they [Trepashkin's sources] had seen the field commander from the brigade of Raduev 'Abdul'.... I also acquainted him with materials relating to 'Abubakar,' who was serving as a 'roof' for a number of sites in the district of the metro *Yugo-zapadnaya*." "Running ahead," Trepashkin added, "I will say that presently I am being accused of, at the end of July and the beginning of August 2002, providing Shebalin with information concerning agents of the FSB of the Russian Federation." Trepashkin's conclusion: "Either the concentration of extremists took place under the control of the Russian FSB and they therefore decided to turn my citing of such information into the revealing of a state secret of Russia, or Shebalin did not transmit the information to the Russian FSB." But Shebalin, it emerged, had indeed transmitted the information. According to the same July statement by Trepashkin: "He [Shebalin] said that the Russian FSB was aware of the information, but as to why they did not undertake any measures, and why, in relation to me, on the contrary, they opened a criminal case and seized the data base I had been collecting for years, including data about terrorists, he did not know."

Moreover, once Trepashkin learned that "Abubakar" was among the hostage takers at Dubrovka, "I again proposed to Shebalin to call up the materials on my computer which had been seized." But "the experts from the Russian FSB deemed the information I possessed about the events at the 'Nord-Ost' to be a state secret of Russia, and I was charged with having revealed a state secret."

On 22 October 2003, Trepashkin was arrested by the Interior Ministry on a highway in Moscow Oblast and charged with transporting a concealed and

---

[25]   "Ekho 'Nord-Osta' i vzryvov domov v Rossii," *Kavkazskii vestnik* (editor@kvestnik.org), 22 July 2003. The text also appeared in: "'Nord-Ost': provokatsiya FSB," Chechenpress.com, 21 July 2003.

unregistered pistol in his car. Trepashkin was able to get out the information that the pistol (supposedly stolen in Chechnya) had been planted in his car and that the regular police had admitted to him that they had acted at the behest of the FSB. Duma Deputy Sergei Kovalev commented concerning this incident: "I do not believe that Mikhail Ivanovich [Trepashkin] had a pistol with him. He is an experienced man, a former officer of the KGB. He is not a bandit, and he is not a fool."[26] On the day preceding his arrest, it might be noted, Trepashkin had granted a major interview to a correspondent for *Moskovskie novosti.*[27]

The Nominal Leader of the Terrorists

A young man who called himself Movsar Baraev served as the titular leader of the group of terrorists that took control of the Moscow theater. Movsar Baraev—who also went by the names Mansur Salamov and Movsar Suleimenov[28]—had but a single claim to fame: He was the nephew of the late Chechen Wahhabi kidnapper and murderer Arbi Baraev. According to a report appearing in the military newspaper *Krasnaya zvezda*, Arbi Baraev "had personally participated in the murder of 170 persons."[29] Nonetheless, Baraev, Movsar's uncle, "had moved freely about the [Chechen] republic showing at federal checkpoints the documents of an officer of the Russian MVD [Interior Ministry]."[30] "On the windshield of [Arbi] Baraev's vehicle," journalist Anna Politkovskaya has noted, "there was a pass, regularly renewed, which stated that the driver was free 'to go everywhere'—the most cherished and re-

---

26   Polina Shershneva, "On poidet do kontsa," Newizv.ru, 24 October 2003.

27   Igor Korol'kov, "Fotorobot ne pervoi svezhesti," *Moskovskie novosti*, 11 November 2003. In the 4 December 2003 issue of *Novaya gazeta*, journalist Anna Politkovskaya reported that Trepashkin was being tried in a closed trial conducted by the Moscow District Military Court and that Amnesty International was in process of according him the status of political prisoner.

28   Vadim Rechkalov, "Vdovii bunt," Izvestia.ru, 25 October 2002; and Lobanova, "Tolko on otvetit za Nord-Ost." See also "Passport terrorista," Izvestia.ru, 24 October 2003.

29   *Krasnaya zvezda*, 26 June 2001.

30   Sanobar Shermatova, "Glavnyi rabototorgovets," *Moskovskie novosti*, 29 October 2002.

spected pass in the Combined Group of [Russian] Forces."[31] Arbi Baraev also had reported shadowy ties to both the Federal Security Service (FSB) and the Russian Military Intelligence (GRU).[32]

In January 2003, a well-known French journalist, Anne Nivat, author of the book *Chienne de Guerre: A Woman Reporter Behind the Lines of the War in Chechnya* (New York, NY: PublicAffairs, 2001), who had conducted a number of incognito visits to Chechnya, reported: "Two months before the hostage taking, the GRU, the secret service of the Russian army, had announced [Movsar] Baraev's arrest. The implication is that he would have been held until his 'arrest' to lead the hostage taking at the Dubrovka theater."[33]

Good reasons exist to doubt that Movsar was the actual leader of the group. "Under his [Movsar Baraev's] control," Sanobar Shermatova has stipulated, "were [only] five to six rebels, and he never demonstrated either the military or organizational abilities necessary for a commander.... The Chechens [sources of *Moskovskie novosti*] say that Baraev himself was not fully initiated into the plan [to seize the theater]. He was supposed to play his role and then burn up like a rocket booster." The former pro-Moscow head of the Chechen Interior Ministry, also a former FSB officer, Said-Selim Peshkhoev "proposed that this group of terrorists was led not by Movsar Baraev but by another person."[34]

Further testimony that Movsar was not the real leader comes from Shamil Basaev. In late April 2003, Basaev recalled: "I included [Movsar] Baraev in this group only in late September [2002]. I had only two hours to talk to him and give instructions."[35] If Movsar Baraev was at this time in the custody of the GRU (as Nivat's sources claim), then Basaev could only have met with

---

31   *Novaya gazeta*, 28 June 2001.
32   Sanobar Shermatova, "Tainaya voina spetssluzhb," *Moskovskie novosti*, 8 August 2000.
33   Anne Nivat, "Chechnya: Brutality and Indifference," Crimesofwar.org, 6 January 2003.
34   Shermatova, "Glavnyi rabototorgovets."
35   Kavkaz-Tsentr News Agency, 26 April 2003.

Baraev through the good offices of that elite organization. Such a scenario is not unimaginable. It is known that Basaev himself worked closely with a purported GRU officer named Anton Surikov when Basaev was serving as deputy defense minister of the separatist (from Georgia) republic of Abkhazia in 1992-93. During the course of a 2001 interview, Surikov assessed "extremely positively" Basaev's role in that conflict.[36] "In the beginning of the 1990s," Surikov affirmed, "he [Basaev] was materially supported by us."

A number of Russian journalists and political analysts have expressed their belief that Basaev and Surikov met together once again some years later— this time together with the chief of the Russian presidential administration, Aleksandr Voloshin, at the estate of a Saudi international arms dealer in southern France in July 1999, in order to seal an agreement which led to Basaev's invasion of Dagestan the following month.[37] In the summer of 2000, when the newspaper *Versiya* published an article about the alleged meeting complete with a group photograph of Voloshin, Basaev, and Surikov, the paper approached Surikov and he "rather severely" told its correspondents to leave him alone. However, Surikov did not deny that the meeting took place. Moreover, almost a year later, when asked about the possible role of the security forces in organizing the invasion of Dagestan, Surikov replied somewhat mysteriously: "A positive answer to your question would sound unproven, although, in my view, such a perspective on events in part has a right to existence, but only in part." Among the more prominent individuals who have voiced this perspective was the former secretary of the Russian Security Council, retired General Aleksandr Lebed. He affirmed his belief in October of

---

36   "Tainyi sovetnik VPK," *Zavtra*, 1 June 2001. At the time of this interview, Surikov was serving as head of the State Duma's Department on Industry. On Surikov, see also: Maksim Kalashnikov, "Chelovek, kotoryi verboval Basaeva," Stringer-news.ru, 10 July 2002.

37   See Petr Pryanshnikov, "Voloshin i Basaev na lazurnom beregu: foto na pamyat," *Versiya*, 4 July 2000. This article can be found at: http:www.compromat.ru/main/voloshin/basaev.htm. See also: Andrei Batumskii, "Sgovor," *Versiya*, 3 August 1999.

1999 that "Basaev and the Kremlin had concluded an agreement," which had led to the August 1999 invasion of Dagestan.[38]

Among the suicide bombers who were present in the Moscow theater, Nivat has also reported, there were two women, who, like Movsar Baraev, had already been placed under arrest by the federal authorities: "At Assinovskaya, a village close to the border with Ingushetiya, which is where two of the [Baraev] unit's women came from, their mothers say they had been arrested [by the Russian authorities] and taken to an unknown destination at the end of September [2002]. Secretive in the presence of the outsider that I am, and still considerably shocked, they won't say more."

In a similar vein, in January 2003, the late Duma Deputy and journalist Yurii Shchekochikhin wrote in the newspaper *Novaya gazeta*:

> Unexpectedly, last week I learned that one of the female terrorists in the Nord-Ost building was not just anyone but a woman who had been imprisoned for a long time in one of the Russian [penal] colonies. She was recognized on television by her mother, a resident of Shelkovskii Raion in Chechnya. She cannot understand how her daughter reached Moscow as a terrorist from a prison cell.[39]

In addition, the well-connected investigative journalist Aleksandr Khinshtein has reported that some eight of the women suicide bombers were able to take up residence in a former "military city" [*gorodok*] in Moscow, located on Ilovaiskaya Street, not far from the Dubrovka theater. This complex, which housed a large number of illegal residents prepared to pay bribes to the authorities, was apparently under the protection of corrupt elements among the Moscow police.[40]

---

[38] "Doslovno," *Novaya gazeta*, No. 37, 4-10 October 1999, 3. Lebed's statement originally appeared in the French newspaper *Le Figaro* on 29 September 1999.

[39] Yurii Shchekochikhin, "Nezamechennye novosti nedeli kotorye menya udivili," *Novaya gazeta*, No. 4, 20 January 2003.

[40] Aleksandr Khinshtein, "Chernye vdovy pod 'kryshei' Petrovki," *Moskovskii komsomolets*, 23 July 2003.

The Active Phase of the Operation Begins

By mid-October 2002, the terrorists had shifted over to the active phase of their operation. During a face-to-face meeting with "Abubakar," Aslambek Khaskhanov learned that "Shamil Basaev had ordered him [Abubakar] to prepare 'a very large action' with a seizure of hostages."[41] The action referred to was, of course, the taking of the theater at Dubrovka.

A series of powerful explosions had been set to go off, beginning on 19 October 2002, with the hostage-taking episode itself having originally been planned for 7 November, the former anniversary of the Bolshevik revolution. Several vehicles were fitted with explosive devices, most likely at the terrorist base at Chernoe in Moscow Oblast, and then moved to a garage at 95 *Leninskii prospekt*. "An explosion [at a McDonald's restaurant in southwest Moscow] took place on 19 October, at approximately 1:05 p.m., that is not during rush hour and not in the most crowded area of the city." This account by the former chief procurator of Moscow, Mikhail Avdyukov, continues: "Two other vehicles [fitted with explosives] were also parked: one next to the Tchaikovsky Theater Hall on *Triumfal'naya* Square, the other near a busy subway transit point in the center. But the more powerful explosives [contained in these two vehicles] did not work."[42] According to one version, the watch mechanism failed to work in the vehicle that had been parked at the Tchaikovsky Concert Hall.

On 20 October, Aslambek Khaskhanov, who had placed the explosives in the three vehicles, flew from Moscow to Nazran, Ingushetiya, using false documents. His decision to leave town has been assessed by one journalist as being due to "banal cowardice." On that same day, his confederate, "Abubakar," according to one report, removed the large bomb from the vehicle at the

---

41   Statement of Moscow's chief procurator Mikhail Avdyukov in "V Moskve gotovilos' chetyre 'Nord-Osta'."

42   *Ibid.*

Tchaikovsky Theater." On 23 October, that bomb was then "placed in the house of culture at Dubrovka."[43]

This powerful bomb placed in the theater, it was later revealed, was in fact incapable of detonating: "The power [ministries] have admitted," *Kommersant* reported in July 2003,

> that the most powerful of the homemade bombs which were placed by the Baraevites in the seized theater center at Dubrovka were not in a condition in which they could be detonated. They lacked such important elements as batteries, which made the bombs harmless *bolvanki* [dummies]. And it was precisely this circumstance that permitted the conducting of a completely successful storm of the theater center.[44]

According to one press report, the powerful bombs placed by Khaskhanov did not go off because of a key design failure. Two of the vehicles that had failed to explode were later located by the Moscow Criminal Investigations Department (MUR) (in January 2003 in a parking lot located off the Zvenigorod Highway), who determined the reason for the failure of the bombs:

> The gas tanks of the vehicles were divided hermetically into two parts: in one half was gasoline while the other was filled with a substance similar to plastic explosive together with nails and fragments of steel barbed wire. However, an examination showed that the amount of plastic explosive was so small that even if an explosion had happened, the explosive force would have been insignificant.[45]

(As we have seen, other reports mention a faulty timing mechanism in the bombs.)

---

[43]   Khinshtein, "Glavnyi terrorist 'Nord-Osta'."

[44]   Otdel prestupnosti, "U terroristov problemy so vzryvchatkoi," *Kommersant*, 7 July 2003. The same claim is made in Sergei Topol, Aleksandr Zheglov, Olga Allenova, "Antrakt posle terakta," *Kommersant*, 23 October 2003.

[45]   Otdel prestupnosti, "U terroristov problemy so vzryvchatkoi."

The explosion of the small bomb contained in the *Tavriya* vehicle that had been parked next to McDonald's restaurant on Porkryshkin Street and had resulted in the death of one person attracted the attention of a unit of MUR, an elite police body designed to combat organized crime and terrorism, commanded by Colonel Yevgenii Taratorin. "The police learned that the *Tavriya* vehicle that had been blown up had been sold by proxy to a certain Artur Kashinskii...whose real name turned out to be Aslan Murdalov, a native of Urus-Martan in Chechnya, who had been living in Moscow for 10 years."[46] Working quickly, the MUR identified Murdalov and took him into custody on 22 October.

It was the arrest of Murdalov that forced the terrorists "to accelerate their activities and the seizure of the hostages at Dubrovka, which had first been planned for 7 November."[47] As journalist Zinaida Lobanova has noted: "The original seizure of the musical 'Nord-Ost' was planned for 7 November, the day of Accord and Reconciliation [the postcommunist name for the holiday], and that seizure was to have been preceded by the explosion of cars in the center of the capital, in order to sow panic."[48] On 22 October, "A.S. Mezhiev informed Abubakar about the taking into custody of A.M. Murdalov.... [Abubakar] told him that in the next few days a powerful operation would take place."[49]

The failure of the two car bombs to explode in crowded locations in the center of the capital required the terrorists to speed up and to alter their plans. The hostage-taking operation at Dubrovka had been intended (at least, apparently, by certain of its planners) to be the culmination of a terror bombing campaign directly reminiscent of the one visited on the capital in September of 1999. Deprived of this sanguinary "introduction," the October 23 hostage-

---

[46] Khinshtein, "Glavnyi terrorist 'Nord-Osta'," Khinshtein's source for this information was officers of the MUR.

[47] Statement of Colonel Taratorin over Russian central television: Leonid Berres, "MUR opravdalsya za 'Nord-Ost'," Izvestia.ru, 7 February 2003.

[48] Lobanova, "Tolko on otvetit za Nord-Ost."

[49] Khinshtein, "Glavnyi terrorist 'Nord-Osta'."

taking action commenced shorn of its spectacular first act. The MUR had gotten on the trail of the terrorists and their associates sooner than had been expected. (In this sense, the entire episode bears a certain resemblance to the well-known Ryazan incident of September 1999, in which the local police interfered with an operation that was under way.[50]). Once the theater had been taken over by the terrorists on 23 October, the officers of the MUR realized that "the terror act at McDonald's and the seizure of the Nord-Ost had been prepared by one and the same people." On 28 October, just two days after the theater had been stormed by Russian special forces units, the MUR took the two Mezhiev brothers into custody.[51]

To return to 23 October—the day on which the Moscow theater was seized by the terrorists—shortly before the raid occurred:

> Abubakar designated a meeting with [Akhyad] Mezhiev near the Crystal Casino. Abubakar was at the wheel of a Ford Transit [minibus]. He handed over to Mezhiev two Chechen girls on whom suicide belts with explosives had been attached. Abubakar ordered that the girls be taken to a populated place where they could blow themselves up and thus draw the attention of the law-enforcement organs away from the seizure of the House of Culture [at Dubrovka].[52]

"At first," the account continues, "Mezhiev decided to let the suicide women off at the Pyramid Cafe, but, having learned by radio of the seizure of the House of Culture, he exhibited cowardice."

---

[50]   On this episode, see Chapter 5 "Proval FSB v Ryazani," in Aleksandr Litvinenko and Yurii Feltshtinskii, *FSB vzryvaet Rossiyu* (Internet Edition, 2002). English translation: *Blowing Up Russia: Terror from Within* (New York: S.P.I. Books, 2002), 62-104. See also Aleksandr Litvinenko, "Ryazanskii sled," Chapter 10 in his *LPG (Lubyanskaya prestupnaya gruppirovka)* (Internet Edition, 2003).

[51]   Khinshtein, "Glavnyi terrorist 'Nord-Osta'."

[52]   *Ibid.* Khinshtein identified Abubakar as being Ruslan Elmurzaev, 30 years old, a native of Urus-Martan in Chechnya, and a former Russian police employee. Subsequently the procurator of Moscow confirmed most of this information, noting also that Elmurzaev's patronymic is Abu-Khasanovich: "V Moskve gotovilos' chetyre 'Nord-Osta'."

A bomb blast at this normally crowded cafe located in the very center of Moscow would have been a catastrophic event. In his taped confession to the police, Akhyad Mezhiev related that, on the night of 23-24 October, Abubakar called him on his mobile phone and demanded angrily: "Why has there been no wedding?" Wedding was "the code word for the designated stage of the terrorist act. Women-bombs was what they had in mind." "Abubakar wanted me," Mezhiev continued, "to send the girls that same night. They had everything ready. Everything depended on me." Mezhiev drove the suicide bombers to the Pyramid Cafe on Pushkin Square. "Here there were always a lot of people. The 'brides of Allah' were to blow themselves up in the crowd." Mezhiev, however, "did not let the women out of the vehicle. Why? We don't know."[53]

Mezhiev then relates (on the police videotape) how he took the belts away from the would-be suicide bombers and then drove them to a train station where he bought them tickets to Nazran, Ingushetiya, and bade them farewell. He then gave the "martyrs' belts" to his brother Alikhan, who, at the command of Abubakar, handed them over to Khampash Sobraliev, one of the two terrorists based in the village of Chernoe in Moscow Oblast.[54] "In a telephone conversation with Abubakar, he [Mezhiev] said that he was afraid and wanted to leave town." This he proved unable to do, and on 28 October he was placed under arrest by the MUR. "He was 'caught out' because of his telephone conversations with Abubakar."[55]

An alternative explanation to the version Mezhiev recounted to the police would be that the women terrorists in fact had been let out of the vehicle but their "martyr-belts" had failed to detonate. Shamil Basaev seemed to allude to such a development in his already-cited statement posted on *Kavkaz Tsentr* on 26 April 2003: "The detonators of our martyrs had not worked: this occurred with those who were inside [the theater at Dubrovka] and four female martyrs who were outside. They returned here. I personally talked to three

---

[53]   Lobanova, "Tolko on otvetit za Nord-Ost."
[54]   *Ibid.*
[55]   *Ibid.*

and they claimed that their detonators had not worked."[56] It is entirely possible, however, that Basaev was aware that the belts would not work and was merely embellishing his tale for the sake of potential donors in the Gulf states and the Muslim world.

"According to the information of the FSB," the newspaper *Kommersant* reported on 29 October,

> the entire building [at Dubrovka] was mined, and the explosion of only a part of the bombs could have brought about the collapse of the theater building. But only a pair of the bombs that were contained in the belts of women-kamikaze exploded. At the moment of the explosion, they [the women] were outside the hall guarding the approach to it. It turns out that all the other bombs were either fakes or they had not been readied for use. For example, they lacked batteries or a detonator.[57]

One of the Russian emergency workers who entered the building after it was stormed by the special forces, Yurii Pugachev, has recalled: "Personally I saw the bodies of several women in black clothing whose stomachs had literally been blown apart. Evidently the explosive was not very strong."[58] "If one is to believe the sources of *Moskovskie novosti*," Sanobar Shermatova and Aleksandr Teit wrote in an article appearing in April 2003, "several of the women suicide fighters, having understood that gas had been let into the hall, tried to connect the lead wires on their suicide belts. They didn't work, because, instead of explosives, there was a fake there. Was that really the way it really was?"[59]

Shamil Basaev has claimed that the original targets of the terrorists were the buildings of the Russian State Duma and the Federation Council. In an article

---

[56]   Kavkaz Tsentr News Agency, 26 April 2003.
[57]   Sergei Dyupin, Aleksei Gerasimov and Leonid Berres, "Zakhvat zalozhnikov v Moskve," *Kommersant*, 29 October 2002.
[58]   Sergei Dyupin, "Peredozirovka," *Kommersant*, 28 October 2002.
[59]   Sanobar Shermatova and Aleksandr Teit, "Shestero iz baraevskikh," *Moskovskie novosti*, 29 April 2003.

appearing in an underground rebel newspaper, *Ichkeriya* Basaev even "provides the measurements of the vestibules of the two buildings."[60] Since, however, Basaev is a habitual distorter of the truth, one must at this point must remain agnostic about what precise building(s) the terrorists intended to target first.

The Russian authorities, it has also been reported, had been forewarned of the impending terrorist attack by none other than the U.S. Central Intelligence Agency (CIA). According to Duma Deputy Yurii Shchekochikhin, he was telephoned on 25 October 2002 by "a high-ranking individual in Washington," who told him that, during the first half of October, the CIA had alerted the Russian government that "a new Budennovsk [a reference to the southern Russian town attacked in June of 1995 by a force headed by Shamil Basaev] was being prepared in Moscow."[61]

In April 2003, there occurred a brief flap when a dissident former FSB officer, Aleksandr Litvinenko, living in London, and a leading Russian journalist, Anna Politkovskaya, reported that an FSB agent of Chechen nationality, Khampash Terkibaev, had been present inside the theater building but had left it before the storming of 26 October.[62] Politkovskaya went on to publish the text of an interview with Terkibaev in which he confirmed that he had indeed been in the building. It emerged, however, that both Litvinenko and Politkovskaya had fallen into an extremely intricate and clever trap, evidently laid by for them by the FSB. Terkibaev, a murky adventurer with almost certain links to the secret police, had boasted during a visit to Baku that he had been in the building at Dubrovka, but he had evidently been lying. Sanobar Shermatova and a co-author pointed out on the pages of *Moskovskie novosti* that Terkibaev, "who in 2000 even found a way to receive a document of amnesty in the FSB office in the city of Argun," had for a number of years been engaging in anti-

---

[60]   Sanobar Shermatova, "'Nord-Ost' ne planirovalsya?" *Moskovskie novosti*, 24 June 2003.

[61]   Yurii Shchekochikhin, "TsRU predupredilo," *Novaya gazeta*, 28 October 2002.

[62]   See "Litvinenko: Yushenkova ubili za rassledovanie terakta v 'Nord-Oste'," Lenta.ru, 25 April 2003 and Anna Politkovskaya, "Odin iz grupppy terroristov utselel. My ego nashli," *Novaya gazeta*, 28 April 2003.

Wahhabi activities and would not therefore have been acceptable to the Movsar Baraev/Abubakar group. "Terkibaev," they noted, "does not deny that after the events around 'Nord-Ost,' he introduced himself in Baku as a participant in the seizure of the hostages."[63]

Another Chechen, Zaurbek Talikhigov, was arrested by the police following the storming of the theater building. He was apparently a walk-on volunteer who, using a borrowed cell phone, attempted to inform the terrorists from outside the building where the Russian forces were positioned. His phone conversations were, of course, monitored and taped by Russian law-enforcement authorities.[64]

The Terrorist Assault on 23 October

On 23 October, shortly after 9:00 p.m., 40 Chechen terrorists whose titular leader was Movsar Baraev—but whose de facto leader was the shadowy "Abubakar" (Ruslan El'murzaev)—stormed (there were no armed guards present so the task was not overly difficult) and took control of the House of Culture at Dubrovka in Moscow, which was putting on the popular musical "Nord-Ost." A total of 979 people were taken captive (there were slightly more than 900 present in the building at the time that it was taken back on 26 October).[65] According to a statement made by the former procurator of Moscow, the terrorists were carrying 17 automatic weapons and 20 pistols, as well as

---

[63] Sanobar Shermatova and Aleksandr Teit, "Antivakhkhabitskii emissar," *Moskvo-vskie novosti*," 13 May 2003. Terkibaev was killed on 15 December 2003 in an automobile crash that some commentators found to be suspicious. "The double agent Terkibaev was removed as a dangerous witness," the website Newsru.com observed on 16 December 2003.

[64] "Posobnik terroristov ne uspel spasti zalozhnikov," *Kommersant*, 11 June 2003.

[65] Grani.ru, 28 November 2002. The website provided a list of the names of 979 individuals taken captive on 23 October. As of 25 October, 58 of the captives had been released. (*The Moscow Times*, 26 October 2002).

various homemade bombs, suicide belts, and grenades.[66] Twenty-one of the terrorists were men and 19 women.[67] As opposed to the "terror bombings" in Moscow in 1999—when the announced suspects had been ethnic Karachai —on this occasion there could be little doubt that the perpetrators were ethnic Chechens, though elements among the hostage takers, with the likely support of the special services involved in the operation, sought to convey the impression that there were Arab terrorists among them.

One website, Utro.ru, which on occasion elects to convey the views of the Russian secret services, focused attention upon one of the terrorists, the mysterious "Yasir" (another name, as we have seen, used by "Abubakar"): "As Utro has learned from sources in the Russian special services," the website wrote,

> there were several rebels who were non-Chechens, including an Arab called (his code-name) Yasir. About him the following is known: this international terrorist is a subject of the kingdom of Saudi Arabia and is on the international wanted list. Yasir entered into the leading link of the cells of 'Al-Qaeda'.... The Wahhabi Movsar Baraev...was in fact a marionette in the hands of experienced puppeteers.[68]

When a deputy minister of the interior, Vladimir Vasilev, was asked by RTR television on 26 October: "Abubakar is an Arabic name, isn't it?" he replied misleadingly: "Naturally, it is."[69] Even one year after the Dubrovka episode, some Russian security officials were continuing to push the fictional "Yasir's" involvement in the hostage-taking events: "The investigation," Gzt.ru reported

---

[66]   "V Moskve gotovilos' chetyre 'Nord-Osta'." A 41st terrorist, the procurator noted, turned out to be an ethnic Russian, the father of one of the hostages, who had foolishly entered the theater on 25 October and had then been shot by the terrorists.

[67]   "Genprokuratura ustanovila imena 33-kh terroristov, zakhvativshikh zalozhnikov v Moskve," Newsru.com, 6 November 2002. Seven remained unidentified as of October 2003.

[68]   Oleg Petrovksii, "V bande Baraeva byl terrorist iz 'Al-Kaedy'," Utro.ru, 30 October 2002.

[69]   "Moskva, zalozhniki," Vesti7.ru, 2 November 2002. This program was broadcast on 26 October.

on 23 October 2003, "has not yet established the identity of a mercenary, an Arab who called himself Yasir. He was using a Russian Federation [internal] passport in the name of Alkhazurov, Idris Makhmudovich, born 1974."[70] One day after the publishing of this information, however, the newspaper *Izvestiya* reported that it had been the titular leader of the terrorists, Movsar Baraev, who in fact had been carrying "a passport in the name of Idris Alkhazurov."[71]

On 24 October 2002, the day following the seizure of the theater at Dubrovka, it was reported by the media that President Vladimir Putin "sees the seizure of the hostages in Moscow as one of the links in a chain of the manifestations of international terrorism, in one row with the [recent] terrorist acts in Indonesia and the Philippines. 'These same people also planned the terrorist act in Moscow,' said Putin."[72]

These "Arab" and "radical Islamic" themes were also heavily accented by the hostage takers themselves. At 10:00 p.m. on 23 October, just 50 minutes after the taking of the building:

> The [former] minister of propaganda of the Ichkerian republic [i.e., Chechnya], Movladi Udugov, speaks to the BBC Service of Central Asia and the Caucasus. He confirms that the group of field commander [Movsar] Baraev organized the hostage taking. According to Udugov, the group consists of kamikaze terrorists and about 40 [sic] widows of Chechen rebels who are not going to surrender. The building is mined.[73]

Udugov was at the time widely believed to be living in Qatar or another of the Gulf states. Two hours later, a website associated with Udugov, *Kavkaz-Tsentr* (Kavkaz.org), reported the same information, adding: "The terrorists are demanding the withdrawal of [Russian] troops from Chechnya.[74]

---

70   "Polnyi spisok opoznannykh terroristov," Gzt.ru, 23 October 2003.

71   Vladimir Demchenko, "Passport terrorista," Izvestia.ru, 24 October 2003.

72   Newsru.com, 24 October 2002.

73   Gzt.ru, 25 October 2002. Item posted in English.

74   Newsru.com, 24 October 2002. The item was reported at 00:04 a.m. on 24 October.

The following day, 24 October, it was reported by the website Gazeta.ru, as well as by other media, that: "The Qatar television company Al-Jazeera broadcast a tape of the Chechen rebels in which they state that they are prepared to die for the independence of their homeland and to deprive of life the hostages located in the building in the theater center." "For us," the hostage takers affirmed on the tape, "it is a matter if indifference where we die." "We have chosen to die here, in Moscow, and we will take with us the souls of the unfaithful," added one of the five women in masks standing in the frame under the sign, "'Allah akbar!' written in Arabic." In another fragment, one of the rebels is shown declaring, "Each of us is prepared for self-sacrifice, for the sake of Allah and the independence of Chechnya."[75] The veiled women were shown dressed entirely in black. Al-Jazeera television also showed one of the male rebels "seated in front of a laptop with the holy Muslim book the Koran by his side." "We seek death more than you seek life," said the man, who was also dressed in black. "We came to the Russian capital to stop the war or die for the sake of Allah," he asserted.[76] Al Jazeera reported subsequently that the interview had been taped on 23 October in Moscow shortly before the Chechens had assaulted the theater.[77]

The rebels also exhibited a militant radical Muslim stance over the course of the few interviews that they granted to Russian and Western media. As NTV correspondent Sergei Dedukh reported on 25 October (the footage was shown the following day): "The two girls in black whom the rebels called their sisters have explosives on their belts with wires sticking out of them. Could you please tell us what your clothes and the explosives in your belt mean?" An unidentified woman hostage taker replied: "They mean that we shall not stop at anything or anywhere. We are on Allah's way. If we die here, that won't be the end of it. There are many of us, and it will go on."[78] Movsar Baraev is then quoted by Dedukh as asserting that "the terrorists' only and fi-

---

[75]   Gazeta.ru, 24 October 2002.
[76]   "Jazeera Shows Taped Chechen Rebel Statements," Reuters, 24 October 2002.
[77]   Associated Press, 26 October 2002.
[78]   "Russian NTV Shows Previously Filmed Interview with Hostage Takers' Leader," *BBC Monitoring Service*, 26 October 2002.

nal goal is the end of the military operation in Chechnya and the withdrawal of [Russian] federal troops."

In an interview with journalist Mark Franchetti of London's *The Sunday Times* Abubakar is quoted as saying: "We are a suicide group. Here we have bombs and rockets and mines. Our women suicide bombers have their fingers on the detonator at all times. Time is running out.... Let the Russians just try to storm the building. That's all we are waiting for. We cherish death more than you do life." When he was finally allowed to interview Baraev, Franchetti witnessed this scene: "Baraev and his men paraded three Chechen women dressed in black with headscarves covering all but their eyes. In one hand each held a pistol, in the other a detonator linked to a short wire attached to 5 kilograms of explosive strapped to her stomach. Except for a beam of light from inside the auditorium, the foyer was dark. One of Baraev's men used a torch to show off the explosives belts. "They work in shifts," explained Baraev. "Those on duty have their finger on the detonator at all times. One push of the button and they will explode. The auditorium is mined, all wired up with heavy explosives. Just let the Russians try to break in and the whole place will explode."[79] (These statements, as we have seen, were an apparent bluff by the terrorist leaders—the explosives were not in reality in a condition in which they could be detonated.)

Putin and his team, manifestly, now had an 11 September 2001 of their own, though it remains unclear whether or not they had been surprised by this development. Signs in Arabic, the brandishing of the Koran, veiled women suicide bombers dressed all in black—what more could the Russian leadership need? Moreover, as distinct from 1999, the terrorists on this occasion were unquestionably Chechens, except, perhaps, for a sprinkling of Arabs such as the fictional "Yasir." The seizing of the theater building, it was heavy-handedly suggested, constituted a link in a chain leading back to the infamous Al-Qaeda.

---

[79]   Mark Franchetti, "Dream of Martyrdom," *The Sunday Times*, 27 October 2002.

Blackening Maskhadov

In addition to seeking to depict the hostage-taking incident as a second 9/11, a second aim behind the regime's response to the crisis appeared to be to fully discredit Aslan Maskhadov, and thus render the possibility of negotiations with him or other moderate Chechen separatists unthinkable. Early on the morning of 25 October, the website Newsru.com (affiliated with NTV) reported: "There has come information that the order to seize the hostages was given by Aslan Maskhadov. One of the Chechen terrorists stated this. A tape of [Maskhadov's] declaration was shown by the channel Al-Jazeera. In it Maskhadov says, 'In the very near future, we will conduct an operation which will overturn the history of the Chechen war.'"[80]

This statement by Maskhadov was cited later on the same day by official spokesmen for both the FSB and the Interior Ministry as self-evident proof of his responsibility for the raid. On 31 October, Putin spokesman Sergei Yastrzhembskii emphasized at a news conference that there could be no question of holding future talks with Maskhadov. "Maskhadov can no longer be considered a legitimate representative of this resistance," Yastrzhembskii told reporters. "We have to wipe out the commanders of the movement," including Maskhadov, he stressed.[81]

This aggressive campaign by the Russian leadership seems to have borne significant diplomatic fruit. On 30 October, the *Los Angeles Times* reported that "a senior U.S. official" in Moscow had termed Maskhadov "damaged goods" with links to terrorism. The senior official went on to assert that "the Chechen leader should be excluded from peace talks."[82] In more judicious fashion, one influential Russian democrat and parliamentary faction leader, Grigorii Yavlinskii, confided on 27 October "his view of Maskhadov has

---

[80] Newsru.com, 27 October 2002.

[81] "Russia Seeks to 'Wipe Out' Chechen Leaders," *Reuters*, 31 October 2002.

[82] Robyn Dixon and David Holley, "U.S. Rejects Chechen Separatist Chief," *Los Angeles Times*, 30 October 2002.

changed. If Maskhadov commanded the rebels in the theater, he said, he could never participate in a political settlement."[83]

But how strong was the evidence linking Maskhadov to the terrorist action? Journalist Mikhail Falkov looked into the issue of the tape of Maskhadov's statement that had been shown over Al-Jazeera and learned that: "Russian television viewers had been presented only with a fragment of the original tape. On the tape it was distinctly evident that the filming had been conducted not in October but toward the end of the summer." This discovery appeared to back up the claim of Maskhadov's official spokesman in Europe, Akhmed Zakaev, that "the question [in Maskhadov's taped statement] concerned not the seizure of hostages but a military operation against federal forces."[84] It should also be noted that, on 24 October, the day following the hostage taking at Dubrovka, Zakaev had written to Lord Judd of the Parliamentary Assembly of the Council of Europe and unambiguously declared: "The Chechen leadership headed by President A. Maskhadov decisively condemns all actions against the civilian population. We don't accept the terrorist method for the solution of any kind of problems.... We call on both sides, both the armed people in the theater and the government of Russia, to find an un-bloody exit from this difficult situation."[85]

In an article appearing in *Moskovskie novosti* journalists Shermatova and Teit reported that a careful analysis of a hushed conversation that had been conducted in Chechen between Abubakar and Movsar Baraev and had been accidentally captured by NTV on 25 October showed the following:

> Here is Movsar Baraev answering the questions of NTV correspondents before a television camera. Next to him stands a rebel, known as Abubakar: he in an undertone in Chechen corrects Movsar. When Baraev declares that they had been

[83]   Sharon LaFraniere, "Setback Seen for Rebel Cause," *The Washington Post*, 28 October 2002.
[84]   Mikhail Falkov, "Kto i gde gotovil moskovskii terakt?" Utro.ru, 31 October 2002.
[85]   "Chechen Press Release on Moscow Hostage Crisis," Chechenpress.com, 24 October 2002.

sent by Shamil Basaev, Abubakar quietly suggests, 'Pacha ch'ogo al,' 'point to the president.' After that, Movsar obediently adds: 'Aslan Maskhadov.'"[86]

Abubakar thus sought publicly to tie Maskhadov directly to the hostage-taking incident.

That Abubakar and not Movsar Baraev was the de facto leader of the terrorists also becomes clear from Franchetti's report: "At one point he [Baraev] lowered his guard. Perhaps succumbing to the lure of fame, he offered to let me film the hostages in the auditorium. His right-hand man [Abubakar] fiercely disagreed.... They briefly left the storage room to confer in the dark foyer.... Baraev came back. There would be no more filming."[87] Abubakar had prevailed over Baraev in a test of wills.

It seems that Abubakar may also in a subtle way have been involved in helping the federal forces to prepare the storming of the theater. "Several sources in the special services," the newspaper *Moskovskii komsomolets* reported on 28 October, "have informed us that in the juice which the negotiators took to the hostages, without their knowledge, there was admixed a substance which was to soften the toxic action of the gas."[88] Abubakar himself raised this topic. Summing up one of her discussion/negotiations with Abubakar, journalist Politkovskaya has recalled: "We agree that I will start bringing water into the building. Bakar suddenly throws in, on his own initiative, 'And you can bring juice.' I ask him if I can also bring food for the children being held inside, but he refuses."[89]

---

[86]   Shermatova and Teit, "Shestero iz baraevskikh." The transcript reads: "[Movsar Baraev]: 'We are acting on orders from the supreme military emir. Our supreme military emir there is Shamil Basaev. You know him very well. And Maskhadov is our president.'" ("Russian NTV shows...," *BBC Monitoring Service*, 26 October 2002.)

[87]   Franchetti, "Dream of Martyrdom."

[88]   "Gibel' zalozhnikov—rezul'tat oshibki spetssluzhb?" *Moskovskii komsomolets*, 28 October 2002.

[89]   Anna Politkovskaya, "My Hours Inside the Moscow Theater," *Institute for War and Peace Reporting*, No. 153, 31 October 2002.

A leading journalist writing on the pages of *Moskovskie novosti*, Valerii Vyzhutovich, looked into the issue of Maskhadov's supposed responsibility for the raid and concluded: "There are no direct proofs convicting Maskhadov of the preparation of the terrorist act in Moscow." He added that "not a single court, not even ours, the most humane and just," would uphold the admissibility in a trial of the edited and highly selective footage shown over Al-Jazeera television—"a propagandistic soporific"—in Vyzhutovich's words.[90]

When Politkovskaya, in a one-on-one private conversation with Abubakar, directly asked him, "Do you submit to Maskhadov?" he replied, "Yes, Maskhadov is our president, but we are making war by ourselves." "But you are aware," she pressed him, "that Ilyas Akhmadov [a separatist spokesman loyal to Maskhadov] is conducting peace negotiations in America and Akhmed Zakaev in Europe, and that they are representatives of Maskhadov. Perhaps you would like to be connected with them right now? Or let me dial them for you." "What is this about?" Abubakar retorted angrily. "They don't suit us. They are conducting those negotiations slowly...while we are dying in the forests. We are sick of them."[91] Abubakar's feelings concerning Maskhadov and other Chechen separatist moderates are revealed in these words.

The regime, for its part, seems to have concluded that it now possessed ample, indeed overwhelming, evidence to prove to both Russian citizens and to Western leaders two key points: first, that the hostage takers were dangerous and repugnant international terrorists in the Al-Qaeda mold; and, second, that the leader of the separatist Chechens, Aslan Maskhadov, had been irretrievably discredited by the raid, rendering the possibility of any future negotiations with him unthinkable.

---

[90]   Valerii Vyzhutovich, "Usyplayushchii gaz," *Moskovskie novosti*, 29 October 2002.
[91]   Anna Politkovskaya, "Tsena razgovorov," *Novaya gazeta*, No. 80, 28 October 2002.

Negotiations Leading Nowhere

The failure of three of the four bombs to detonate confronted both the terrorists and the Russian authorities with an exceedingly slippery situation. How was the crisis to be resolved? Abubakar reluctantly consented to conducting a series of negotiations with various Duma deputies, journalists, and at least one doctor, while the Russian power ministries for their part set about practicing a raid on the theater building. Duma deputies who, at great personal risk, visited the building in order to negotiate with the terrorists were: Yabloko faction leader Grigorii Yavlinskii; Aslambek Aslakhanov, the parliamentary deputy representing Chechnya; Irina Khadamada; Iosif Kobzon; and Vyacheslav Igrunov. (Another Duma faction leader, Boris Nemtsov of the Union of Rightist Forces, negotiated with the terrorists by telephone.) Also visiting the building were former Russian Prime Minister Yevgenii Primakov and the former president of Ingushetiya, Ruslan Aushev. A key role was, as we have seen, played in the negotiations by journalist Anna Politkovskaya. Doctor Leonid Roshal, who treated the hostages, and Sergei Govorukhin, the son of a famous Russian filmmaker and himself a Chechen war veteran, also attempted to facilitate the negotiations.[92]

Yavlinskii's experience with the negotiations has been summarized thus:

> The hostage takers were said to have asked specifically for Yavlinskii.... He said he met with the hostage takers for an hour and a half on the night of 24 October. They said they wanted an end to the war in Chechnya and the withdrawal of federal troops, but Yavlinskii said when he tried to get them to formulate their demands, they were unable to come up with any kind of a coherent negotiating position. 'Let's go step by step. You want a cease-fire, OK, let's go for a cease-fire,' Yav-

---

[92] For a list of the negotiators, see "Te, kto ne strelyal," *Moskovskie novosti*, 29 October 2002. The presence of the name of Sergei Dedukh here is incorrect; he visited the theater in the capacity of a correspondent for NTV. The information concerning Igrunov's visit appeared in *Gazeta Wyborcza* (Poland), 24 October 2002, posted at Chechnya-sl@yahoogroups.com, 24 October 2002. Politkovksaya paid tribute to Aslakhanov's role in "Posle 57 chasov," *Novaya gazeta*, No. 82, 4 November 2002.

linskii said he told the hostage takers. 'Tell me which regions to pull troops out of. Tell me something I can use.'[93]

"I insisted," Nemtsov confided to *Nezavisimaya gazeta*,

> that we had maximally to move the negotiation process forward with a single goal—to free the children and women. And my logic—about which both Patrushev and Voloshin knew—and I stated it also to Abubakar, the *politruk* [political officer] of the terrorists responsible for the negotiations, was the following: for each peaceful day in Chechnya they would release hostages. One peaceful day—the children; another one—the women, and so on. The rebels liked that idea. And the day before yesterday was indeed a peaceful day. But when I reminded Abubakar about our agreements, he sent me to the devil and said that one should talk with either Basaev or Maskhadov.[94]

"There are five requests," Politkovskaya has recalled,

> on my list. Food for the hostages, personal hygiene for the women, water and blankets. Jumping ahead a little, we will only manage to agree on water and juice.... I begin to ask what they want, but, in political terms, Bakar isn't on firm ground. He's 'just a soldier' and nothing more. He explains what it all means to him, at length and precisely, and four points can be identified from what he says. First, [President Vladimir] Putin should 'give the word' and declare the end of the war. Secondly, in the course of a day, he should demonstrate that his words aren't empty by, for example, taking the armed forces out of one region.... Then I ask, 'Whom do you trust? Whose word on the withdrawal of the armed forces would you believe?' It turns out that it's (Council of Europe rapporteur) Lord Judd. And we return to their third point. It's very simple—if the first two points are met, the hostages will

[93] Alex Nicholson, "Yavlinsky Describes His Role in Crisis," *The Moscow Times*, 5 November 2002.

[94] Olga Tropkina, "Vvedenie tsenzury dopustimo," *Nezavisamaya gazeta*, 28 October 2002.

be released. And as for the extremists themselves? 'We'll stay
to fight. We'll die in battle.'[95]

While letting volunteer negotiators such as Politkovskaya buy some time, the
regime limited itself to delivering only a few public messages to the terrorists.
On 25 October, the director of the Federal Security Service (FSB), Nikolai
Patrushev, "declared that the terrorists would be guaranteed their lives if the
hostages...were released. He made this declaration after meeting with Russian President Vladimir Putin." Also on 25 October, at 8:30 in the evening, "the
chair of the Federation Council, Sergei Mironov, addressed the hostages and
terrorists on direct open air on a radio program of *Ekho Moskvy*. Addressing
the terrorists, he [Mironov] declared: 'Advance your real conditions, free our
people, and you will be ensured safety and security to leave the boundaries of
Russia. You have de facto already achieved your goal of attracting attention.
The entire world is talking about it.'"[96] Presented one day before the launching
of the storm, these statements appear to have been another attempt to buy
time.

Late in the evening of that same day, 25 October, the regime offered to begin
serious negotiations on the following day (26 October), with retired General
Viktor Kazantsev, Putin's official representative in the Southern Federal District, meeting with the hostage takers. This gesture came at a time when
preparations for the storm were moving ahead full tilt. The rebels, for their
part, reacted positively to this development, "announcing to the hostages that
they had 'good news.'... Tomorrow [Saturday, 26 October] at 10:00 a.m., Kazantsev will come. Everything will be normal. They have come to an agreement. This suits us. Behave peacefully. We are not beasts. We will not kill you
if you sit quietly and peacefully.'"[97] Political and security affairs correspondent
Pavel Felgengauer has reported that Kazantsev made no preparations to actually fly from southern Russia to Moscow.[98]

---

[95]   Politkovskaya, "My Hours Inside the Moscow Theater."
[96]   Newsru.com, 27 October.
[97]   "Gazeta.ru reskonstruirovala shturm," Gazeta.ru, 28 October 2002.
[98]   Pavel Felgengauer, "'Nord Ost': reputatsiya ili gaz?" *Novaya gazeta*, 27 October
2003.

According to Duma faction leader Yavlinskii, he came to understand "by 5 p.m. on 25 October" that Putin had adopted an irrevocable decision to storm the building.[99] The Gazeta.ru website has reported that, "The first information that a decision concerning a storm had been taken and that it had been set for the morning of 26 October was gained by journalists working in the area of the theater center at about 11:00 p.m. on 25 October."[100] Felgengauer observed over Ekho Moskvy radio on 26 October:

> Our forces...stormed the 'Nord-Ost' building after two days of preparations, without even so much as a prior attempt to negotiate with the captors in any meaningful way to secure a peaceful solution to the affair.... This week, first there was reconnaissance. By every conceivable means of electronic and acoustic surveillance, the terrorists' exchanges and movements were monitored. On Friday [25 October], the plans were reported to Vladimir Putin, who gave the go-ahead for the operation to start on Saturday.[101]

A member of the special forces units which took the building provided support for Felgengauer's interpretation in remarks made to Gzt.ru:

> We put bugs everywhere, even in the concert hall. We accompanied every negotiator; in the beginning we did it openly, but then the Chechens became indignant.... When the journalist, Anna Politkovskaya, made the agreement with them to deliver water, food, and medicine, headquarters had already prepared everything.... Everybody knew about the storm. Only nobody knew when it would happen.[102]

It was the special forces and not the terrorists who appear to have precipitated the final denouement. "At 5:20 a.m. [on 26 October]," journalist Valerii Yakov has written,

---

[99] Nicholson, "Yavlinsky Describes his Role in the Crisis."

[100] "Gazeta.ru rekonstruirovala shturm."

[101] "Russian pundit critical of hostage rescue operation, policy on Chechnya," *Ekho Moskvy Radio, BBC Monitoring Service*, 26 October 2002.

[102] "Feat of Arms," Gzt.ru, 31 October 2002. In English.

the operation suffered its first setback. The terrorists noticed in the building a movement of a group of 'Alfa' [special forces] and opened fire. They were instantly destroyed, but it was necessary immediately to correct the plan [of attack].... At this time, a representative of the FSB, Pavel Kudryavtsev, came out to the journalists and reported that the terrorists had shot two men and that another man and a woman had been wounded. Later it emerged that this information was false.[103]

The above-cited correspondent Felgengauer has, for his part, commented: "There are no serious grounds for these heroic fairy tales [about an execution of the hostages by the terrorists] to be believed. Long before the building was stormed, it had become obvious in many ways that everything would be decided precisely on Saturday morning."[104] The producer of the Nord-Ost musical, Georgii Vasilev, who was the de facto leader and chief spokesman for the hostages, declared: "I have heard that they began the storm supposedly because they [the terrorists] began to execute the hostages. That is the official point of view of the authorities. I want to say that there were no executions—only threats."[105]

As is well known, a decision was taken by the Russian authorities to employ a powerful gas in the retaking of the building. As one military affairs specialist, Viktor Baranets, has reported,

the idea of using gas during the operation to liberate the hostages was in the heads of many members of the operational headquarters already during the second day of the emergency situation when it became clear that they would hardly come to agreement with the terrorists.... It was decided to use the most powerful poison [available]—a psycho-chemical gas (PChG).

---

[103] Valerii Yakov, "My vse zalozhniki Kremlya," *Novye izvestiya*, 29 October 2002. See also: "Two Hostages Killed in Moscow Theater," AP, 26 October 2002, posted at 4:52 a.m.
[104] "Russian pundit critical of hostage rescue operation, policy on Chechnya."
[105] "Tri dnya v adu," *Komsomol'skaya pravda*, 29 October 2002.

According to some sources, it has the name 'Kolokol [i.e., Bell]-1.'[106]

What was in this gas? "We are never going to know exactly what chemical it was," Lev Fedorov, an environmental activist who is the head of the Russian Union for Chemical Safety, has aptly commented, "because in this country the state is more important than the people."[107]

According to the website Gazeta.ru, the special forces began pumping gas into the hall through the ventilation system at 4:30 a.m., "a half an hour before the storm."[108] Other sources contend, however, that it may have been significantly earlier, perhaps shortly after 1:00 a.m.[109] One possibility is that a decision was taken to strengthen the dosage of the gas after the initial infusion did not seem to be having the desired effect. The chief anesthesiologist of Moscow, Yevgenii Evdokimov, has speculated: "The death of those people was possibly caused by an overdose of the substance [in the gas]."[110] The website Gzt.ru wrote on 28 October: "It has become known to Gazeta that the first attempt to neutralize the bandits located among the hostages did not succeed—the concentration of the poisonous substance turned out to be insufficient."[111]

According to an October 2003 statement by the press department of the Moscow City Prosecutor's Office, 125 hostages died from the effects of the gas, some of them following the storm while they were in hospital, while five were

---

[106]   Viktor Baranets, "Komanda-shturm!" *Komsomol'skaya pravda*, 29 October 2002.

[107]   Cited in Susan B. Glasser and Peter Baker, "Gas in Raid Killed 115 Hostages," *The Washington Post*, 28 October 2002.

[108]   "Gazeta.ru rekonstruirovala shturm."

[109]   Gazeta.ru, 31 October 2002. Testimony of hostage Aleksandr Zeltserman, a resident of Latvia. The accounts of special forces personnel who participated in the storming suggest that they began letting in the gas at about 1:15 a.m. See "Ofitsery 'Alfy' i 'Vympela' o shturme," Gzt.ru, 30 October 2002. The article "Kreml' nameren skryt' pravdu o terakte na Dubrovke," Apn.ru, 1 November 2002 states that they began pouring in the gas "at about 2:30 a.m. on 26 October—that is, approximately three hours (!!) before the storm."

[110]   Dyupin, "Peredozirovka."

[111]   "Osvobozhdenie: neizvestnye podrobnosti," Gzt.ru, 28 October 2002.

killed by the terrorists.[112] The actual death toll from the effects of the gas might, according to some estimates, have in fact exceeded 200.[113] In addition, scores of other hostages were reported at the time to be seriously ill from the effects of the gas.[114] In April 2003, a lawyer representing some of the former hostages asserted that approximately 40 more of the hostages had died since 26 October 2002.[115] In October 2003, the newspaper *Versiya*, summing up the results of an investigation conducted by its journalists, stipulated that "about 300" of the former hostages were now dead.[116] The incompetence and the disorganization of the medical and emergency teams called in to treat the ill and the dying were unquestionably a cause of many of the deaths. The medical teams, in their defense, had not been informed about what was in the gas. When the Russian State Duma declined to carry out an inquiry into the actions of the medical teams, the Union of Rightist Forces conducted its own investigation and then published its scathing findings.[117]

At 8:00 a.m. on 26 October, one hour after the building had been declared liberated, Russian state television (RTR) showed the following mendacious tableau:

---

[112] Topol, Zheglov and Allenova, "Antrakt posle terakta." A year previously, Andrei Seltsovskii, chair of the Moscow Committee on Health, had stated that "only two [hostages] died of gunshot wounds." ("Peredozirovka.")

[113] I stipulated the number 204 in my "Taking a New Look at the Hostage-Taking Incident," *Chechnya Weekly*, 17 December 2002. Julius Strauss, who had been in an apartment building with a clear view of the main entrance to the theater, wrote in "Kremlin Keeping Siege Deaths Secret to Avoid Criticism," *The Daily Telegraph*, 31 October 2002: "There are now fears that the final death figure, if it is ever published, may be above 200." The website Utro.ru reported on 28 October 2002 that 160 hostages had already died and that 40 were in the hospital in such a grave condition and that they could not be saved.

[114] Judith Ingram, "Moscow Theater Hostages Face Poor Health," Associated Press, 6 December 2002.

[115] Margarita Kondrateva, "Zhertvy 'Nord-Osta' provodyat nezavisimoe rassledovanie," Gzt.ru, 28 April 2003.

[116] *Versiya*, 21 October 2003.

[117] See "Duma says no to theater terrorism inquiry," Gazeta.ru, 1 November 2002. For the text of the Union of Rightist Forces' report, see "Kak eto bylo? Spasenie zalozhnikov ili unichtozhenie terroristov?" *Novaya gazeta*, No. 86, 21 November 2002.

The gang leader [Movsar Baraev] met his death with a bottle of brandy in his hand. According to special-purpose-unit men, they found an enormous number of used syringes and empty alcohol bottles on the premises. The criminals, who described themselves as champions of Islam and freedom fighters, must have spent the last hours in the theater bar. Even the women, officers say, smelt strongly of alcohol. Probably because of that,... [the women terrorists] did not have time to set in motion the explosive devices attached to their waists. According to specialists, each device contains at least 800 grams of TNT. Besides, in order to increase the impact, the devices were filled with ball bearings and nails. Another explosive device was planted in the center of the hall, which, to all appearances, was intended to make the ceiling collapse. And there is a whole arsenal on the stage: assault rifles, TNT, cartridges. And the most interesting are these homemade grenades. Despite their small size, they are extremely powerful.[118]

(By this time, if not earlier, the Russian authorities must have become fully aware that the explosives placed in the hall had been incapable of detonating.)

On 27 October, President Putin invited the special forces commandos from the *Al'fa* and *Vympel'* units who had taken back the theater to a special reception at the Kremlin. In his remarks, Putin praised the professionalism of the two units of the FSB, and he then joined with them in a silent standing toast.[119] In early January 2003, shortly after New Year's Eve, "Putin signed a secret decree to award six people with Hero of Russia stars, including three FSB officials and two soldiers from the special units 'Alfa' and 'Vympel.' The sixth 'hero' is the chemist who gassed the theater center."[120]

---

[118] "Empty alcohol bottles, syringes found inside Moscow siege building," RTR, *BBC Monitoring Service*, 8:00 a.m., 26 October 2002.

[119] "Putin priglasil v Kreml' 'Alfu' i 'Vympel'," *Komsomol'skaya pravda*, 1 November 2002.

[120] Vladimir Kovalev, "Russia: Heroes and Lawyers," *Transitions Online*, http://www.tol.cz, 10 March 2003. See also Yurii Shchekochikhin, "Sekretnye geroi," *Novaya gazeta*, No. 16, 3 March 2003.

Following the storming of the theater building, the president's approval ratings for his conduct of the war in Chechnya shot up in the polls: "If in September, 34 percent of Russian citizens had been in favor of continuing military actions, while 56 percent had favored peace negotiations, at the end of October—for the first time since the beginning of 2001—the opinions divided almost half and half: 46 percent were for military actions, while 45 percent were for negotiations."[121]

Questions

From the testimony of former hostages interviewed by the Russian media, it seems virtually certain that the terrorists did have ample time to destroy many of the hostages before they themselves had been overcome by the gas or shot by the attacking special forces. Why did they not do so? As we have seen, most of the explosives in the building were "fakes" or very weak bombs presenting a danger principally to the women terrorists wearing them. Even without detonating the bombs, however, the terrorists carried real automatic weapons and could easily have raked the hostages with automatic-weapon fire. They clearly chose, however, to let the hostages live. Even an Interior Ministry general who had been identified by the terrorists and had been separated from the other hostages was not killed (though his daughter died from the effects of the gas).[122] Theater producer Vasilev has recalled: "When the shooting began, they [the terrorists] told us to lean forward in the theater seats and cover our heads behind the seats."[123]

How many of the terrorists were killed in the raid? In June 2003, Moscow City Prosecutor Mikhail Avdyukov stipulated that a total of 40 terrorists had been killed and that none had managed to escape.[124] The same figure was given by Avdyukov's successors in October 2003.[125] At 9:44 a.m. on 26 October

---

[121] Yurii Levada, "Reiting voiny," *Novoe vremya*, 5 November 2002.

[122] Testimony of hostage Ilya Lysak, in *Novaya gazeta*, 14 November 2002.

[123] Reuters, 27 October 2002.

[124] "V Moskve gotovilos chetyre 'Nord-Osta'."

[125] Topol, Zheglov and Allenova, "Antrakt posle terakta."

2002, however—that is, almost three hours after the building had been declared liberated—it was reported by Interfax that only 32 terrorists had been
killed. The same day, the director of the FSB, Nikolai Patrushev, affirmed that
"34 gunmen were killed and an unspecified number arrested."[126] By contrast,
on 28 October, Gzt.ru, a "centrist" publication, reported that "50 terrorists—32
men and 18 women" had been killed and "three others taken into custody."[127]
The compromise figure of 40 dead terrorists was arrived at later.

A number of questions have been asked by analysts and journalists about
whether or not the de facto leader of the terrorists, Abubakar, had in fact been
killed. In June 2003, Moscow Prosecutor Avdyukov insisted that Ruslan Abu-
Khasanovich Elmurzaev's body had been found and identified.[128] In March
2003, however, retired FSB Lieutenant Colonel Mikhail Trepashkin had written that, following the events at Dubrovka, "I proposed to the investigators
that they try to identify 'Abubakar' in the first days after the event. However,
later an investigator telephoned and said that he could not find the corpses of
a number of people, including that of 'Abubakar,' and therefore there would
be no identification."[129] And journalist Aleksandr Khinshtein has reported: "At
first there existed a version that Abubakar died during the storming of the
House of Culture.... But a series of examinations showed that there was no
Abubakar in the hall."[130] Despite Prosecutor Avdyukov's statement, it appears
thus to be an open question as to whether or not Abubakar was killed.

In October 2003, film director Sergei Govoroukhin, one of the volunteer negotiators who had spoken at length with Abubakar at Dubrovka, stated his belief
that Abubakar was still alive. Despite his persistent requests, he said, Russian prosecutors had proved unable to show him Abubakar's body. "Moreover," Govorukhin continued,

---

[126] "Russian Security Service Says No Gunmen Escape," AP, 26 October 2002.

[127] "Osvobozhdenie: neizvestnye podrobnosti."

[128] "V Moskve gotovilos chetyre 'Nord-Osta."

[129] Trepashkin, "Spravka," 23 March 2003. Lengthy excerpts from this document were
published in "Tainstvennyi 'Abubakar'." On 27 December 2003, the website Grani.ru
published a statement by Mikhail Trepashkin, which had been smuggled out of
prison, in which he asserted that he was being physically tortured by the authorities.

[130] *Moskovskii komsomolets*, 23 May 2003.

two weeks ago, during a trip to Chechnya, I asked intelligence [officers] of the Combined Group of Forces of the Northern Caucasus whether it was true that Abubakar was in Chechnya. I was uniformly given the same answer: 'Of course he is here. He has shown himself rather actively in recent times, and only for the past month has nothing been heard of him.' Therefore I can maintain absolutely accurately that he is alive.[131]

Similarly, also in October 2003, an investigative report appearing in the newspaper *Kommersant* noted that "until the summer of this year [2003], when the case concerning the explosion at a McDonald's restaurant was being investigated by the Procuracy of the western district [*okrug*] of Moscow, Ruslan Elmurzaev was still on the wanted list. He was removed from the wanted list only when the case was taken over by the Moscow [City] Prosecutor's Office."[132] The same report also added this key detail: "As sources in the FSB and [Interior Ministry] have made clear, the terrorists themselves ordered that the bombs [in the Dubrovka theater] be rendered harmless before the seizing of the hostages. Abubakar was supposedly afraid of accidental explosions."[133]

Aftermath of the Hostage-Taking Incident

On the evening of 6 February 2003, a sensation of sorts was created when "the head of the operational-investigative department of the MUR [Moscow Criminal Investigations Office], Yevgenii Taratorin, made an unexpected announcement on the television program 'Man and the Law.'" In Taratorin's words, "In October-November of last year, in addition to seizing the theater center at Dubrovka, the band of Movsar Baraev planned explosions in the Moscow underground, at a popular restaurant, and at the Tchaikovsky Con-

---

131   Zoya Svetova, "Ya uveren, chto Abubakar zhiv..." Ruskur.ru, 23 October 2003.
132   Topol, Zheglov and Allenova, "Antrakt posle terakta."
133   *Ibid.*

cert Hall. In the words of the policeman, the operatives of the capital's criminal-investigation unit were able to avert all of these terrorist acts." Following the explosion of the "Tavriya" car bomb at McDonald's restaurant on Porkryshkin Street in Moscow on 19 October, Taratorin related, the MUR discovered "in the center of Moscow at the Tchaikovsky Concert Hall in direct proximity to the GAI [traffic police] post an automobile of silver color containing explosives." Quick action by the MUR and the arrest of certain of the terrorists, Taratorin claimed, forced the hostage takers to move up the date of their assault on the theater at Dubrovka from 7 November to 23 October.

According to Taratorin, "on 24 October, the operatives averted two other terrorist acts: the explosion of an automobile at the Pyramid [Restaurant] in Pushkin Square and the self-detonation of a female suicide bomber at one of the stations of the capital's underground." The terrorists, sensing the danger of a rapid unmasking, then fled to the North Caucasus region. (Taratorin appears here to be exaggerating the achievements of the MUR: the bombings failed to occur, as we have seen, most likely either because the terrorists "exhibited cowardice" or because the bombs themselves were faulty in design or construction.)

In the course of his televised statement, Taratorin added that, in November 2002, in the village of Chernoe in Moscow Oblast, the police had "discovered a house in which, among apples, there was found ammunition and, next to the cottage, a hiding place in which explosives brought from Ingushetiya had first been concealed."[134] (The explosives, he said, had later been transferred to two garages located on *Leninskii prospekt* and *Ogorodnyi proezd* in Moscow.) In January 2003, Taratorin added, two of the intended car bombs had been found in a parking lot off Zvenigorod Highway.

Most sensationally of all, Taratorin claimed that "five people" in all had been arrested for participating in the terrorist act. Queried about this statement, the Russian Prosecutor-General's Office insisted heatedly that only two persons

---

134   Berres, "MUR opravdalsya za 'Nord-Ost'." See, too, Andrei Skrobot, "V 'Lefortovo' doprashivayut geroev 'Nord-Osta'," *Nezavsimaya gazeta*, 25 June 2003.

had so far been arrested, one of them the walk-on Chechen volunteer Zaur-bek Talikhigov. Journalists soon discovered, however, that "three more Che-chens whom they had connected to Dubrovka had been released last No-vember [2002]."[135]

Following this televised statement by the MUR colonel, "the Procuracy opened against Yevgenii Taratorin a [criminal] case for his having revealed a secret of the investigation. But this did not stop the colonel—in particular, he intended to meet with journalists...in order to relate to them the details of the investigation in the course of which the MUR officers did not succeed in find-ing understanding on the part of the 'neighbors' from the FSB."[136] Taratorin was placed under arrest by the FSB on 23 June 2003, as part of a putative "campaign against werewolves" in the Russian Interior Ministry.[137] This lengthy campaign and media reactions to it strongly suggested that the arrest of Taratorin, like that of Trepashkin, was a selective one triggered solely by the need to silence an official who had begun to expose the fabric of lies that constituted the official version of events.

Taratorin's revelations were embarrassing to the FSB and the Prosecutor-General's Office because they drew attention to the fact that two major sus-pects who had been seized by police at Chernoe on 22 November 2002 had been released: a recently retired GRU major, Arman Menkeev; and a Che-chen originally from Vedeno, Khampash Sobraliev, the man who had col-lected the suicide belts from the women terrorists on 24 October after they had apparently failed to work. "For a long time," however, "Kh. Sobraliev was not charged under Article 205 of the Criminal Code of the Russian Federation (terrorism). This led to his refusal to cooperate with the investigators."[138] In an article appearing in April 2003, journalist Zinaida Lobanova noted that Kham-pash Sobraliev, Arman Menkeev, and Alikhan Mezhiev "were not charged

---

[135]   Berres, "MUR opravdalsya za 'Nord-Ost'."
[136]   Andrei Sal'nikov, "Peredel vnutrennikh del," *Kommersant-dengi*, 7 July 2003.
[137]   Gzt.ru, 24 June 2003.
[138]   Khinshtein, "Glavnyi terrorist 'Nord-Osta'."

and were then set free."[139] Only Akhyad Mezhiev, Alikhan's brother, who had been arrested on 28 October 2002, was still being kept in custody.

When the police raided the terrorist base at Chernoe in November 2002, another of the terrorists, Aslambek Khaskhanov, reportedly managed to escape from the premises. In late April 2003, however, Khaskhanov was located and then arrested in Ingushetiya.

> The Chechen had made his way [from Moscow] to Grozny and concealed himself for almost half a year. At the end of April [2003], he was taken into custody and brought to Moscow. During interrogations he related that in one of the homes on Nosovikhinskii Highway [in Chernoe] were concealed plastic explosives. The operatives arrived with dogs trained to sniff out explosives at House No. 100.[140]

Under interrogation, Khaskhanov reportedly told the police about a huge cache of explosives hidden near the house: 400 kilograms of plastic explosives in total. "'Four hundred kilos of plastic explosives,' whistled one expert. 'That is enough to blow the Kremlin and Red Square to the devil."[141]

In an interview appearing in the government newspaper *Rossiiskaya gazeta* in June 2003, then Moscow City Prosecutor Avdyukov reported that, in addition to Khaskhanov, "Aslan Murdalov, the brothers Alikhan and Akhyad Mezhiev, Khampash Sobraliev, and Arman Menkeev are all now under arrest."[142]

Once Avdyukov and other Moscow prosecutors had been purged from their posts, a "cleansed" Moscow Prosecutor's Office began to surface a new and radically altered version of events. The press office of the Procuracy informed *Kommersant* on 22 October 2003 that five individuals—Aslambek Khaskhanov, Aslan Murdalov, the brothers Alikhan and Akhyad Mezhiev, and Khampash Sobraliev—were now being charged with "belonging to a group which

---

[139] Lobanova, "Tolko on otvetit za 'Nord-Ost'."
[140] Skrobot, "Vzryvy v Moskve gotovyat v Podmoskove."
[141] Lobanova et al., "Naiden ment, pustivshii terroristov v 'Nord-Ost'."
[142] "V Moskve gotovilos chetyre 'Nord-Osta'."

as far back as 2001 had been sent by Shamil Basaev to commit terrorist acts in Moscow."[143] Significantly, retired GRU Major Menkeev was no longer being charged by the Moscow City Prosecutor's Office. Menkeev confirmed this fact to the newspaper *Versiya*, noting that he had been released from prison on 20 October 2003. "I want to say that all charges concerning my participation in a terrorist act have been dropped," Menkeev emphasized.[144]

The version of events being related by the press department of the Moscow City Prosecutor's Office in October 2003 differed in major ways from the former account of the now-purged Mikhail Avdyukov-led Procuracy.[145] According to the new version, "the Urus-Martan Wahhabi [Aslambek] Khaskhanov" had, in the fall of 2001, sent a team consisting of seven rebels to Moscow. Once there, they had purchased three vehicles, one of them a "Tavriya," "which they intended to mine and blow up in parking lots at the buildings of the State Duma [!] and at the McDonald's restaurant at Pushkin Square." The rebels had received plastic explosives "from persons who have not been identified by investigators." It emerged, however, that the plastic explosive employed by the rebels was in fact "imitation plastic explosive" which originally had "a Ministry of Defense origin." "It is fully possible," the account continued, "that the imitation plastic explosive was provided to the terrorists of Khaskhanov by the former employee of the GRU, Major Arman Menkeev, a specialist in explosive substances." Not surprisingly, the account noted, the bombs placed at the building of the State Duma and in Pushkin Square had failed to work. Did this whole operation of 2001—if it in fact occurred—escape official notice completely? This would be quite extraordinary, especially in the wake of 11 September 2001.

"The group of Aslambek Khaskhanov," the revised Moscow City Prosecutor's Office account continued, "came to Moscow a second time, already in the fall of 2002. This time the terrorists also planned to commit a series of explosions

---

143   Topol, Zheglov and Olga Allenova, "Antrakt posle terakta."
144   Irina Borogan, "Obvinyaemogo v tragedii 'Nord-Osta' vypustili na svobodu," *Versiya*, No. 41, October 2003. On Menkeev, see also Aleksandr Elisov, "Zov krovi," Mk.ru, 24 October 2003.
145   Topol, Zheglov and Allenova, "Antrakt posle terakta."

after which, making use of the panic and confusion, one other group of rebels under the command of Movsar Baraev and Ruslan Elmurzaev (Abubakar) was to perform a mass seizure of hostages." On 19 October, the group, using a land mine (*fugas*), set off a car bomb in a *Tavriya* vehicle parked at the McDonald's on Pokryshkin Street. Once the Baraevites had seized the theater building, the Khaskhanov group then chose to go underground.

The new and quite drastically revised version of events currently being put out by the post-purge Moscow City Prosecutor's Office strikes one as, in essence, a complete fabrication. Most of the key discoveries made by the MUR and by the now-"cleansed" former Moscow Procuracy have been adroitly swept under a rug, while Arman Menkeev's role in the events of October 2002 is now passed over in total silence.

Conclusion

Elements among both the Russian leadership and the power ministries and among the Chechen extremists obtained their principal goals in the assault on the theater at Dubrovka: namely, an end was put to the negotiation process while Aslan Maskhadov's reputation was besmirched, and the terrorists, for their part, had an opportunity to stage a grandiose fund-raiser. The Russian authorities, moreover, were now able to demonstrate to the entire world that Moscow, too, had been a victim of an Al-Qaeda-style Chechen terrorist act. As in 1999, the chief victims of these terrorist acts were the average citizens of Moscow. The bulk of the evidence, as we have seen, points to significant collusion having occurred on the part of the Chechen extremists and elements of the Russian leadership in the carrying out of the Dubrovka events.

Bibliographical Update (November 2005)

The following are summaries of noteworthy press items that have appeared in the three years following the tragic events at Dubrovka in October 2002. In September of 2003, the Tverskoi Court in Moscow confirmed an earlier decision reached by the Russian General Procuracy "not to open a criminal case on the illegal use of narcotic substances [i.e., a special gas] in the freeing of the hostages at the Theater Center at Dubrovka."[146] In March of 2004, the Zamoskvoretskii District Court in Moscow in similar fashion declined a request by a Russian human rights organization to open a criminal case on the use of a special gas at Dubrovka.[147]

In February 2004, a closed, secret trial of four accused terrorists charged with bombing a McDonald's restaurant in southwest Moscow opened at the Moscow City Court.[148] The four accused—Alikhan and Akhyad Mezhiev, Aslan Murdalov, and Khanpasha Sobraliev—received prison sentences ranging from fifteen to twenty-two years.[149] Retired GRU major Arman Menkeev was not among those charged with a crime.

In May 2004, the court of the Moscow Military Garrison sentenced lawyer Mikhail Trepashkin to four years in a penal colony. Trepashkin was charged with "revealing a state secret" as well as with "exceeding his authority" and "illegally carrying a weapon."[150]

In October 2004, the newspaper *Izvestiya* reported "that the direct organizer of the terrorist act at Dubrovka was the head of the economic security service at the Prima Bank [in Moscow], Ruslan Elmurzaev, also known as Abu-Bakar.

---

[146] "Sud podtverdil zakonnost' otkaza Genprokuratury vozbudit' delo protiv spetssluzhb," Grani.ru, 30 September 2003.

[147] For the full text of the court's decision, see "Delo 'Nord-Ost'," Hro.org, 3 March 2004

[148] "Nachalsya sud nad organizatorami vzryva u stolichnogo 'Makdonaldsa,'" Izvestia.ru, 25 February 2004.

[149] "Rassledovanie terakata na Dubrovke prodleno na dva mesyatsa," Newsru.com, 22 October 2005.

[150] "Patrony i dissidenty," *Novaya gazeta*, 20 May 2004; "Mikhail Trepashkin vystupil s poslednim slovom," Grani.ru, 17 May 2004.

He received two credits from his bank for $10,000 and $30,000, with which he organized the terrorist act."[151]

In March of 2005, a leading Moscow lawyer, Karina Moskalenko, representing the families of the victims at Dubrovka, announced that "at a minimum 174" hostages had died as a result of the storming of the theater building, not the 129 claimed by the Moscow Procuracy. Moskalenko learned this number by studying documents that had been released to her by the Moscow Procuracy as well as the materials of the court case concerning the terrorist act. Moskalenko reported that 104 hostages perished while in the theater and that the remainder died in the hospital as a result of the effects of the special gas.[152]

In April 2005, the Dmitrovskii Court of Moscow Oblast' added an additional year to the prison sentence of lawyer Mikhail Trepashkin, confirming the charge that he had allegedly been carrying an illegal pistol in his car.[153] In August 2005, Trepashkin was unexpectedly released from prison.[154] The following month, however, he was arrested once again, and he currently remains in prison.[155]

In November 2005, Igor Trunov, a lawyer representing the former hostages and their relatives officially demanded that the Moscow Procuracy "investigate facts of marauding" committed by the secret police, regular police and rescue personnel during the process of removing the bodies of the deceased hostages from the theater building. Significant amounts of money and other valuables were allegedly stolen from the bodies of the deceased. Victims of the terrorist act have, Trunov said, already filed approximately fifty appeals with the procuracy concerning this question.[156]

---

[151] "Nord-Ost zakhvatil bankir," Izvestia.ru, 26 October 2004; see also "Taina sledstviya," Vremya.ru, 25 October 2004.

[152] "Advokat postradavshikh na Dubrovke uznala iz zasekrechennogo dela: v 'Nord-Oste' ubity ne 129, a 174 cheloveka," Newsru.com, 17 March 2005.

[153] "Dopolnitel'noe vremya," Newizv.ru, 18 April 2005.

[154] "Trepashkin osvobozhden uslovno-dosrochno," Grani.ru, 31 August 2005.

[155] "Eks-polkovnik FSB Mikhail Trepashkin osvobozhdennyi iz kolonii, vnov' vzyat pod strazhu," Newsru.com, 18 September 2005.

[156] "Kto obobkral pogibshikh zalozhnikov 'Nord-Osta'?" Gzt.ru, 23 November 2005.

Dr. Andreas Umland (Ed.)

SOVIET AND POST-SOVIET
POLITICS AND SOCIETY

ISSN 1614-3515

This book series makes available, to the academic community and general public, affordable English-, German- and Russian-language scholarly studies of various *empirical* aspects of the recent history and current affairs of the former Soviet bloc. The series features narrowly focused research on a variety of phenomena in Central and Eastern Europe as well as Central Asia and the Caucasus. It highlights, in particular, so far understudied aspects of late Tsarist, Soviet, and post-Soviet political, social, economic and cultural history from 1905 until today. Topics covered within this focus are, among others, political extremism, the history of ideas, religious affairs, higher education, and human rights protection. In addition, the series covers selected aspects of post-Soviet transitions such as economic crisis, civil society formation, and constitutional reform.

SOVIET AND POST-SOVIET POLITICS AND SOCIETY

Edited by Dr. Andreas Umland

ISSN 1614-3515

9   *Алексей Юрьевич Безугольный*
Народы Кавказа в Вооруженных силах СССР в годы Великой Отечественной войны 1941-1945 гг.
С предисловием Николая Бугая
ISBN 3-89821-475-3

10   *Вячеслав Лихачев и Владимир Прибыловский (ред.)*
Русское Национальное Единство, 1990-2000. В 2-х томах
ISBN 3-89821-523-7

11   *Николай Бугай (ред.)*
Народы стран Балтии в условиях сталинизма (1940-е – 1950-е годы)
Документированная история
ISBN 3-89821-525-3

12   *Ingmar Bredies (Hrsg.)*
Zur Anatomie der Orange Revolution in der Ukraine
Wechsel des Elitenregimes oder Triumph des Parlamentarismus?
ISBN 3-89821-524-5

13   *Anastasia V. Mitrofanova*
The Politicization of Russian Orthodoxy
Actors and Ideas
With a foreword by William C. Gay
ISBN 3-89821-481-8

14   *Nathan D. Larson*
Alexander Solzhenitsyn and the Russo-Jewish Question
ISBN 3-89821-483-4

15   *Guido Houben*
Kulturpolitik und Ethnizität
Staatliche Kunstförderung im Russland der neunziger Jahre
Mit einem Vorwort von Gert Weisskirchen
ISBN 3-89821-542-3

16   *Leonid Luks*
Der russische „Sonderweg"?
Aufsätze zur neuesten Geschichte Russlands im europäischen Kontext
ISBN 3-89821-496-6

17   *Евгений Мороз*
История «Мёртвой воды» – от страшной сказки к большой политике
Политическое неоязычество в постсоветской России
ISBN 3-89821-551-2

18   *Александр Верховский и Галина Кожевникова (ред.)*
Этническая и религиозная интолерантность в российских СМИ
Результаты мониторинга 2001-2004 гг.
ISBN 3-89821-569-5

19   *Christian Ganzer*
Sowjetisches Erbe und ukrainische Nation
Das Museum der Geschichte des Zaporoger Kosakentums auf der Insel Chortycja
Mit einem Vorwort von Frank Golczewski
ISBN 3-89821-504-0

Laura Victoir
The Russian Land Estate Today
ISBN 3-89821-426-5

Stephanie Solowyda
Biography of Semen Frank
ISBN 3-89821-457-5

Margaret Dikovitskaya
Arguing with the Photographs
Russian Imperial Colonial Attitudes in Visual Culture
ISBN 3-89821-462-1

Stefan Ihrig
Welche Nation in welcher Geschichte?
Eigen- und Fremdbilder der nationalen Diskurse in der Historiographie und den Geschichtsbüchern in der Republik
Moldova, 1991-2003
ISBN 3-89821-466-4

Sergei M. Plekhanov
Russian Nationalism in the Age of Globalization
ISBN 3-89821-484-2

Михаил Лукянов
Российский консерватизм и реформа, 1905-1917
ISBN 3-89821-503-2

Robert Pyrah
Cultural Memory and Identity
Literature, Criticism and the Theatre in Lviv - Lwow - Lemberg, 1918-1939 and in post-Soviet Ukraine
ISBN 3-89821-505-9

Dmitrij Chmelnizki
Die Architektur Stalins
Ideologie und Stil 1929-1960
ISBN 3-89821-515-6

Andrei Rogatchevski
The National-Bolshevik Party
ISBN 3-89821-532-6

Zenon Victor Wasyliw
Soviet Culture in the Ukrainian Village
The Transformation of Everyday Life and Values, 1921-1928
ISBN 3-89821-536-9

Nele Sass
Das gegenkulturelle Milieu im postsowjetischen Russland
ISBN 3-89821-543-1

Series Subscription

Please enter my subscription to the series *Soviet and Post-Soviet Politics and Society*, ISSN 1614-3515, as follows:

❒ complete series   OR   ❒ English-language titles
                                                            ❒ German-language titles
                                                            ❒ Russian-language titles

starting with
❒ volume # 1
❒ volume # ___
    ❒ please also include the following volumes: #___, ___, ___, ___, ___, ___, ___
❒ the next volume being published
    ❒ please also include the following volumes: #___, ___, ___, ___, ___, ___, ___

❒ 1 copy per volume   OR   ❒ ___ copies per volume

Subscription within Germany:

You will receive every volume at 1st publication at the regular bookseller's price – incl. s & h and VAT.

Payment:

❒ Please bill me for every volume.

❒ Lastschriftverfahren: Ich/wir ermächtige(n) Sie hiermit widerruflich, den Rechnungsbetrag je Band von meinem/unserem folgendem Konto einzuziehen.

Kontoinhaber: _____Kreditinstitut: _____

Kontonummer: _____Bankleitzahl:_____

International Subscription:

Payment (incl. s & h and VAT) in advance for

❒ 10 volumes/copies (€ 319,80)   ❒ 20 volumes/copies (€ 599,80)

❒ 40 volumes/copies (€ 1.099,80)

Please send my books to:

NAME_____DEPARTMENT_____

ADDRESS _____

POST/ZIP CODE_____COUNTRY _____

TELEPHONE _____EMAIL_____

date/signature_____

A hint for librarians in the former Soviet Union: Your academic library might be eligible to receive free-of-cost scholarly literature from Germany via the German Research Foundation. For Russian-language information on this program, see
        http://www.dfg.de/forschungsfoerderung/formulare/download/12_54.pdf.

Please fax to: **0511 / 262 2201 (+49 511 262 2201)**
or mail to: *ibidem*-Verlag, Julius-Leber-Weg 11, D-30457 Hannover, Germany
or send an e-mail: ibidem@ibidem-verlag.de

ibidem-Verlag
Melchiorstr. 15
D-70439 Stuttgart

info@ibidem-verlag.de

www.ibidem-verlag.de
www.edition-noema.de
www.autorenbetreuung.de

Printed in the United States
110614LV00003B/340/A